Prayers for
Strength *and*
Healing

Publications International, Ltd.

Introduction

Sickness, disability, heartsickness, grief: our lives are marked by events that weaken our spirits and our bodies. Our best life experiences—having families, taking risks, making ourselves vulnerable—can cause stress and pain even as they lift us up.

Prayer gives each of us a direct line to God when we need it most, whether for our long-term ailments and troubles or fleeting moments of sickness. He always answers our prayers; we need to learn to hear him.

God, too, can provide us with strength in our must vulnerable moments.

Each page of *Prayers for Strength and Healing* is filled with devotional writings and prayers that can be read quickly whenever you may need them, providing meaningful and contemplative meditations on faith. Each day features a different prayer for every occasion, and the inspiration and guidance you will receive from this book will fortify your relationship with God.

God is present in every situation, from the good to the bad, and it is with prayer that we can ask for his intervention along our journey. We must turn to him if we desire guidance, and it is with prayer that our divine and holy thoughts are transformed into the actions of the follower. God is listening and waiting for us to talk to him.

January

January 1

> *As for God, his way is perfect:*
> *the word of the Lord is tried:*
> *he is a buckler to all those that trust in him.*
>
> —*Psalm* 18:30

Great God, I praise and honor you for keeping your
promises. You have said that you would be with us
always and that you would give us life and peace and
protect us from harm. You have acknowledged that
tough times would come, but you have promised to
meet us there, to share your bountiful resources with
us, to help us through the crises, and to be our refuge.
Thank you, Lord, for being with us.

January 2

> *For the Lord God is a sun and shield:*
> *the Lord will give grace and glory:*
> *no good thing will he withhold from them*
> *that walk uprightly.*
>
> —*Psalm 84:11*

Lord God, help me walk uprightly today—not to impress anyone else or to make myself feel morally superior to those around me. Help me walk uprightly that I might enjoy fellowship with you as you intend it so that nothing may hinder our joy of communing together throughout the day. If others see your light shining in me, may they be drawn to you. If your blessing comes through an act of love or obedience, give me a thankful heart that you have upheld me in your righteousness. Grant me true humility as you teach me to walk in your ways. It is because you are good that I can walk with you!

January 3

Heavenly Father, I'm still not sure I really understand forgiveness. I know all about right and wrong, and I try to do what's right. I see that misbehavior on my part brings bad results. I'm deeply sorry for the sins I've committed, and I know I deserve your punishment. But instead of punishing me, you forgive. You take the penalty upon yourself, and you invite me to live in a loving relationship with you. You have every right to banish me from your presence, but instead you welcome me in. It is truly amazing! Humbly, I thank you.

January 4

I pray for a strong spirit to stand against my fears to-day. I don't ask for fearlessness, because I do feel fear, and I do worry and doubt and I am human. Instead, I pray that you will be at my side in frightening situations, and that you will never leave me abandoned and forgotten. I pray you will shore up my own spirit and give me a sharp mind and deep faith, so that I can overcome any blocks in the road to love, peace, and happiness. Lord, stand beside me, and hold my hand, but also give me that extra bit of courage for the times you ask that I walk through the darkness alone. Thank you, Lord. Amen.

January 5

> *And he shall be like a tree planted
> by the rivers of water,
> that bringeth forth his fruit in his season;
> his leaf also shall not wither;
> and whatsoever he doeth shall prosper.*
>
> —*Psalm 1:3*

Nourishing Lord, I want to grow in you. Let me drink in your goodness and bear spiritual fruit. This is what I was made for, isn't it? To thrive in an ongoing relationship with you? Speak to me as I come before you each day, not only praying but also listening. Instruct me as I read your Word. Guide me as I live each moment. Use other believers to encourage me and steer me in the right direction. Empower me to touch others with your love. I may be just a sapling now, Lord, but I'm growing with your help.

January 6

> *But they that wait upon the Lord shall renew their strength;*
> *they shall mount up with wings as eagles;*
> *they shall run, and not be weary;*
> *and they shall walk, and not faint.*
>
> —Isaiah 40:31

Dear God, your love embraces me like the warmth of the sun, and I am filled with light. Your hope enfolds me in arms so strong, I lack for nothing. Your grace fills me with the strength I need to move through this day. For these gifts you give me, of eternal love, eternal peace, and most of all, for eternal friendship, I thank you God.

January 7

The Lord is my strength and song,
and is become my salvation.
—Psalm 118:14

Lord, my heart was broken, but I know you can fix it. As I learn to depend on you, give me the same thing you gave your servant David: strength and a song. Amen.

January 8

> *Be strong and of a good courage, fear not,*
> *nor be afraid of them: for the Lord thy God,*
> *he it is that doth go with thee;*
> *he will not fail thee, nor forsake thee.*
>
> —Deuteronomy 31:6

Holy Creator, who hath bound together heaven and earth, let me walk through your kingdom comforted and protected by the warm rays of your love. Let me be healed as I stand basking in the divine light of your presence, where strength and hope and joy are found. Let me sit at rest in the valley of your peace, surrounded by the fortress of your loving care.

January 9

Commit thy way unto the Lord;
trust also in him;
and he shall bring it to pass.
—*Psalm 37:5*

January 10

God, I look around my community today and I feel helpless. The homeless, the hurting, the needs each one represents are more than I can handle. But you can do it. You can meet each need. Teach me. Strengthen me and use me to serve as I reach out to my neighbor and meet Just One Need at a Time!

January 11

Only be thou strong and very courageous, that thou mayest observe to do according to all the law, which Moses my servant commanded thee: turn not from it to the right hand or to the left, that thou mayest prosper whithersoever thou goest.

—*Joshua 1:7*

January 12

The Lord will give strength
unto his people;
the Lord will bless his people with peace.

—Psalm 29:11

I am strong as an ox, brave as a lion, and bold as a steer. God's spirit within gives me the strength to move mountains and the courage to go the distance when others have given up. I am powerful in his presence!

January 13

In the dead of winter, God of
springtimes, I'm gardening. Carrot tops rooting, sweet potatoes
vining. I don't doubt the outcome
since I've learned at your knee to
live as if. As if useless can become
useful; as if seemingly dead can live; as
if spring will come. How does a winter
garden grow? With hope, knowing that
you, O God, color even our wintry days
from love's spring palette.

January 14

> *With my whole heart have I sought thee:*
> *O let me not wander*
> *from thy commandments.*
> *Thy word have I hid in mine heart,*
> *that I might not sin against thee.*
>
> —*Psalms 119:10–11*

Practice makes perfect, especially with God. If someone asked, could you list the ten commandments, or explain the context of one of his miracles in the Gospel of John? We often memorize frivolous things without meaning to. Perhaps that energy can be redirected into stoking our love for God.

January 15

> *I exhort therefore, that, first of all,*
> *supplications, prayers, intercessions,*
> *and giving of thanks, be made for all men;*
> *for kings, and for all that are in authority;*
> *that we may lead a quiet and peaceable life*
> *in all godliness and honesty.*
>
> —*1 Timothy 2:1–2*

Life is full of trade-offs, Lord, and I need to make one. Guide my search for a career where I can have both a life and a living. Your balance is not found running in a circle, but along a beckoning path where enough is more than sufficient; where money comes second to family, community, and self; where success takes on new meaning; and where, in the giving up, I gain wealth be-yond belief.

January 16

> *Take therefore no thought for the morrow:*
> *for the morrow shall take thought*
> *for the things of itself.*
> *Sufficient unto the day is the evil thereof.*
>
> —Matthew 6:34

God, so much of life is fleeting. It seems like we are always saying goodbye to this person or that situation. But there is one thing we can always count on—your love. Like the foundation upon which our lives are built, your love gives us stability, something to hold onto when everything around us is whirling chaos. Like the roof over our heads, your love shelters us from life's worst storms. Thank you, God, for your everlasting love.

January 17

Make me strong in body and in spirit.
Give me a faith that never weakens, and
a courage that never wavers. Help me,
Lord, to be a rock to those who need me,
as you always are to me. Help me to also
help myself when no one is around, and to
learn to lean on your wisdom and guid
ance rather than my own. Be my rock and
my shield, guarding me from harm. Amen.

January 18

Deliver me from mine enemies, O my God: defend me from them that rise up against me.

—*Psalm 59:1*

When my enemies rise up against me, almighty Father, I'm tempted to ask you to crush and destroy them. But I pray that you would fill my heart with mercy so that, instead of asking for revenge, I will merely ask with the psalmist that you will rescue and protect me from those who seek to harm me, for I belong to you.

January 19

> *I will go in the strength of the Lord God:*
> *I will make mention of thy righteousness,*
> *even of thine only.*
>
> —*Psalm 71:16*

Holy God, I ask for your righteousness to fill me, thrill me, captivate me, and motivate me. I want a righteousness steeped in your love rather than in my own pride. I want a righteous life that emanates a deep sense of gratitude and not a holier-than-thou attitude. This isn't about me being some sort of spiritual giant. It's about you living your life through me. In Jesus' sacred name, I pray. Amen.

January 20

> *I called upon the Lord in distress:*
> *the Lord answered me,*
> *and set me in a large place.*
>
> —*Psalm 118:5*

It's just a matter of time, sovereign Lord, until each struggle I face passes and I emerge from a place of distress into a place of deliverance and rest.

Help me to never abandon hope in the middle of a trial. May I always press on in prayer, calling out to you, knowing that you hear me and that you are orchestrating the outcome for my eternal good. Hear my prayer even now, for I am calling on you for the deliverance I need this day.

January 21

> *Stir up thyself, and awake to my judgment,*
> *even unto my cause,*
> *my God and my Lord.*
>
> —Psalm 35:23

Sovereign Lord, I need your help. I have come to the end of my own ability. You know the situation I'm in, the problems I'm having, and the obstacles I face. I need a miracle! Please step in to help, I've tried to fix things myself, but I've made things worse. Whenever I forge ahead in my own direction, I do damage. So I'm appealing to you. I need you now. I've always needed you, but now I realize how much.

Don't be a stranger to me. I invite you to step in and work your wonders in my situation. And for whatever I do, I will give you all the glory.

January 22

Great and good Father, increase my concern for those who need practical intervention in their lives and who may need the help of another person to encourage or teach or defend or shelter them in some way. Bring these vulnerable ones to my attention, and though I may not be able to provide everything they need, show me what you would have me offer that would demonstrate your care. Grant me your own compassion and willingness to give of myself for the sake of another. In Jesus' name, I pray. Amen.

January 23

Defend the poor and fatherless:
do justice to the afflicted and needy.
—Psalm 82:3

After you recover from a crisis, you are better able to help others. God strengthened you; now he can use you to strengthen others.

January 24

Lead me, dear Lord. I need your light shining on the road ahead of me. Life is complicated these days, and I don't know where to turn. Illuminate the options for me. Let me see which path to take. I need your truth ringing in my ears. So many voices these days woo me this way or that way, I don't know whom to believe. Except you. I trust your Word, and I trust you to guide me through my current straits.

January 25

> *The Lord liveth; and blessed be my rock;*
> *and let the God of my salvation be exalted.*
> —*Psalm 18:46*

Is there some way today, awesome God, that you can exalt your name through me? A way I might highlight the blessing of your salvation to those around me? I don't want to preach or push or pry in my desire for people to know how wonderful it is to belong to you. I just want to point to you in some encouraging and helpful way. Exalt yourself through me, I pray, in ways you see fit, in ways you know will be a benefit to those you've placed in my life and to those whom you send across my path.

January 26

A father of the fatherless,
and a judge of the widows,
is God in his holy habitation.

—*Psalm* 68:5

Heavenly Father, I think of you, the Father of all creation. Yet I realize that there are all kinds of fathers in this world. Some are absent or abusive; some are distant or demanding; and some are caring and giving. When some people think of you as a father, fear and anger consumes them. But here the psalmist calls you "father of orphans." For anyone who needs a good father, you step in. Whatever failings any earthly father has, you make up for that earthly father. In you, there is genuine fatherly love available to us all. Thank you, my "heavenly dad."

January 27

> *Be of good courage,
> and let us play the men for our people,
> and for the cities of our God:
> and the Lord do that
> which seemeth him good.*
>
> —2 Samuel 10:12

Father, I pray today for a clear path, a strong wind at my back pushing me forward, and the courage of a lion to step into greatness. I am afraid and uncomfortable, but with you I can begin the journey of a thousand miles—with one bold step.

January 28

> *But the Lord is faithful,*
> *who shall stablish you,*
> *and keep you from evil.*
>
> —2 Thessalonians 3:3

We will know when it's time to make our stand. God will speak to us a little louder, a little stronger. The whisper within will become a mighty roar, as we are encouraged to step out in faith and be who God meant us to be.

January 29

Great and glorious God, I live in a culture where mocking and disrespect are the norm, even considered a form of humor. How can I begin to understand what it means to fear you and to have reverence and awe for you? O Lord, teach me what this kind of fear is and what it means in attitude and action. Please open my heart and mind more and more to your thoughts and ways.

January 30

O Lord our Lord,
how excellent is thy name in all the earth!
who hast set thy glory above the heavens.

—*Psalm 8:1*

The queens and kings of earth borrow their majesty from God's hand. No mortal, with all his might, can cause even a blade of grass to grow, and yet the grandeur of the mountains on which the meadows flourish is the result of a few more words spoken by the Lord God!

January 31

I have received rich blessings from you, dear
Lord. I cannot count the ways you have blessed me. But now I'm invited to bless you. I love
the idea that I can bring you joy by praising
you, by thanking you, and by serving you. Let
me pay you compliments for your creativity,
wisdom, and patience. I love you, Lord, and
I'm deeply grateful that you are my Lord.

February

February 1

> *The Lord God is my strength,*
> *and he will make my feet like hinds' feet,*
> *and he will make me to walk*
> *upon mine high places.*
>
> —Habakkuk 3:19

Even in our toughest moments, Lord, we yearn to grow into fullest flower. Give us a faith as resilient and determined as dandelions pushing up through cracks in the pavement.

February 2

> *He healeth the broken in heart,*
> *and bindeth up their wounds.*
>
> —*Psalm 147:3*

The pain of losing someone dear to us or watching a relationship come to an end can be overwhelming. We feel bereft and alone, confused and lost, certain that we will hurt like this forever. But with God's strength, we can move on.

February 3

My Lord, sometimes I feel all alone, as if no one really knows what I'm going through or no one cares. Yes, there are people in my life, and some of them treat me nicely, but there are times when even their kindnesses aren't enough. I feel isolated, abandoned, up against overwhelming obstacles with little or no support. You have seen my affliction. You understand my adversity. In your divine knowledge, you know exactly what's going on, and you promise me your steadfast love. Even before anything changes, it's a comfort to know that you know. It's a blessing to sense your presence beside me. And now I ask for your strength to overcome any obstacle.

February 4

> Truly my soul waiteth upon God:
> from him *cometh* my salvation.
> He only *is* my rock and my salvation;
> he is my defence; I shall not be greatly moved.
>
> —Psalm 62:1–2

Sometimes, Lord, I just need to get away from it all—
to be quiet and rest. Thank you for providing a place
of rest. Life spins so quickly that I can't always
keep up. I start to worry about what
might happen. Those worries then
add stress to my life, affecting the
way I work and the way I relate to
others. Friendships get frayed,
mistakes get made, and I
have even more to worry
about. So right now I'm
quieting down, and I'm
turning to you for help. I
trust you to provide the
deliverance I need.

February 5

> *I laid me down and slept;*
> *I awaked; for the Lord sustained me.*
>
> —*Psalm 3:5*

At least! What a day it has been! I thought I'd never get to this moment, dear Lord. Thank you for the ways you were there for me today. I really sensed your presence throughout the day. Please work things out for me tomorrow, too. And please give me a good night's sleep. Let's talk again in the morning. Amen.

February 6

I can do all things through Christ which strengtheneth me.

—Philippians 4:13

Father, when I don't have another ounce of strength to give, you give me gallons of love to fuel my spirit. When I think I can't continue, you push me further and steady my steps. Thank you, God.

February 7

> For thus saith the Lord God,
> the Holy One of Israel;
> In returning and rest shall ye be saved;
> in quietness and in confidence
> shall be your strength:
> and ye would not.
>
> —Isaiah 30:15

God, sometimes I wish I could be saved from the struggle and pain of learning the hard way. But, Lord, that's not your plan, and I need to be willing to wait as you work gently from the inside out. Please grant me some strength in this time of uncertainty. I trust and love you. Amen.

February 8

Why standest thou afar off, O Lord?
why hidest thou *thyself* in times of trouble?

—*Psalm 10:1*

February 9

Claudia is a painter. When a college friend reached out and suggested that the two of them meet weekly over lunch, she was excited. She thought that the meals would be a nice break from her studio work. But she soon discovered that the lunches were draining, mired in gossip and negative talk. As a result, her mood, and her productivity, suffered. "I discontinued the lunches," she said simply. "They weren't good for my painting— or for me."

Dear God, may I not be distracted from my goals; please help me to block out petty problems and gossip!

February 10

God, I pray for the strength and the wisdom to know what to do in this situation. I pray for enough love to forgive this person for the pain they have caused me and to forgive myself for the ill will I have harbored against this person. Help me be a truly forgiving person so that the weight of resentment may be lifted from my shoulders. Amen.

February 11

You are my King, O Lord. Blessed be your name. I magnify you, telling of your greatness. You rule the earth with your loving power. You dwell in your people and whisper words of peace and guidance. You are immense and intimate at the same time, the Creator of all, yet friend to the needy. I will praise you as long as I live.

February 12

I humbly bow before your throne,
Ashamed of things that I have done.
How could you ever look at me again?
My promises have come to naught.
I haven't lived the way I ought. That's not a fitting
way to treat a friend. I will not dare to seek your face.
I plead for mercy, love, and grace. Perhaps you could
restore some tiny part?
You lift me up and take my hand,
With words I'll never understand.
And let forgiveness flower from your heart.

February 13

> *I will praise the Lord*
> *according to his righteousness:*
> *and will sing praise*
> *to the name of the Lord most high.*
> —*Psalm 7:17*

Along with the psalmist, Lord, I thank you. You have blessed my life richly, and I live each day in gratitude. Each breath I take is a gift from you. Each move I make stems from the power you bestow. All I am and all I have belong to you. Accept the expressions of my heart as songs of praise to you, my great and loving Lord. Let my entire life be an offering to you.

February 14

> *But the scripture hath concluded all under sin, that the promise by faith of Jesus Christ might be given to them that believe.*
>
> —Galatians 3:22

My faith in you fortifies me, and gives me strength. My faith in you is like nourishment when I am hungry or water when I am thirsty. It gives me life and energy and hope. My faith in you overcomes all fears, doubts, and insecurities, knowing that it isn't me doing the work, but you working through me. My faith in you is life-sustaining and creates miracles big and small everywhere I go. The results of my faith in you, Lord, are the abundant blessings you shower upon me for simply believing and trusting in you. Amen.

February 15

In the day when I cried thou answeredst me,
and strengthenedst me
with strength in my soul.

—Psalm 138:3

God, give me the insight to discern your will for me.
Help me to ignore those who may not have my best
interests at heart. Give me strength to stay on my
own path until I achieve my goals.

February 16

> *The name of the Lord is a strong tower:*
> *the righteous runneth into it, and is safe.*
> —*Proverbs 18:10*

I pray today for your mercy and compassion. I'm struggling with life, wrestling against it and not allowing you to work your miracles through me. I pray for a release from the blocks that keep me from your love and guidance. I pray for a stronger, deeper faith in the perfection of my life, even if I can't make sense of it right now. I pray for more spiritual endurance and fortitude when I feel like giving up. I pray, God, for your constant and loving presence. Amen.

February 17

Were there skeptics in your childhood math classes
who asked questions like, "How can infinity plus one
still be infinity?" The fact of the Trinity is a cause for
awe and wonder, not skepticism.

February 18

> But *let it be* the hidden man of the heart,
> in that which is not corruptible,
> *even the ornament* of a meek and quiet spirit,
> which is in the sight of God of great price.
>
> —*1* Peter 3:4

The seasons have meaning with our quiet loved ones. In spring, we weed the beds and plant the flowers. In fall, we pick the peaches, apples, and berries. In winter, we bundle up in afghans before the fire, reading, sharing, and laughing, with bellies full of warming meals. When spring returns, daffodil bulbs poke up their shoots through softening earth. As we work together and nurture one another, our love grows.

February 19

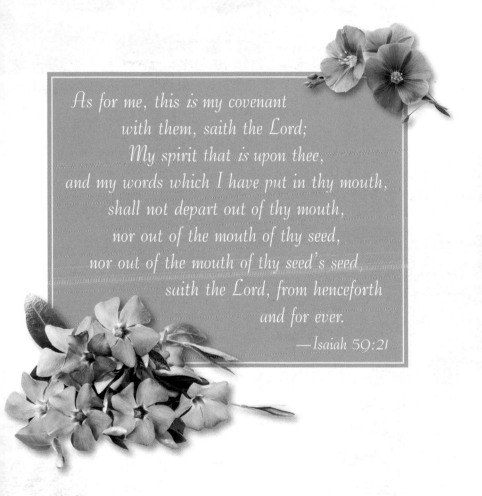

As for me, this *is* my covenant
with them, saith the Lord;
My spirit that *is* upon thee,
and my words which I have put in thy mouth,
shall not depart out of thy mouth,
nor out of the mouth of thy seed,
nor out of the mouth of thy seed's seed,
saith the Lord, from henceforth
and for ever.

—Isaiah 59:21

February 20

Like the evergreen, hope never dies, but stands tall and mighty against the coldest winter winds until the summer sun returns to warm its outstretched branches.

February 21

*Because he hath set his love upon me,
therefore will I deliver him:
I will set him on high,
because he hath known my name.*

—Psalm 91:14

February 22

That he would grant you,
according to the riches of his glory,
to be strengthened with might
by his Spirit in the inner man.

—*Ephesians 3:16*

The strength of an angel is purity.
Truth be known, this is the strength
of each of us.

February 23

*This is a faithful saying,
and worthy of all acceptation,
that Christ Jesus came into the world
to save sinners; of whom I am chief.*

—1 Timothy 1:15

Lord, today, a little white lie slipped out of my mouth to save me from trying commitment. As soon as I felt your little tug on my conscience, I knew I had to come clean about it and repair my relationship with you and with my friend. I know that the lie wasn't small in your eyes, and it was a reminder to me that I am always vulnerable to sin. If I didn't feel your nudge to repair the situation as quickly as possible, I might have fallen into a complacency that would make me vulnerable to any number of more serious sins. I thank you for nudging me, Lord, and for forgiving me, yet again.

February 24

For I long to see you, that I may impart
unto you some spiritual gift,
to the end ye may be established;
that is, that I may be comforted together with
you by the mutual faith both of you and me.

—Romans 1:11–12

Almighty God, of all the things you've created, friendship must be among your favorites. What a joy it is for me to be with my girlfriends, Lord. What encouragement and affirmation I get from them—and what correction if it's needed! I cried when one of my dearest friends told me she was moving two states away, but you, O Lord, have kept us close in heart. That's the beauty of true friendship. It isn't just for here and now. It's forever.

February 25

My flesh and my heart faileth:
but God is the strength of my heart,
and my portion for ever.

—*Psalm 73:26*

Lord, just when I was thinking I was
too pooped to get through the day,
I heard a praise song on the radio. It
reminded me of the unending supply of
energy and strength that is ours through
faith in you! Thanks for getting me
through the day today, Lord. I would be
so lost without you.

February 26

Are there graces for lettuce, Lord? And low-fat, no-fat, meat-free, fun-free meals? I need you to send me words for blessing this paltry meal, for it's hard to feel grateful for these skimpy portions when all I think of are the foods not on my plate. Help me change that thought, to make peace with choosing not to eat them, for I need help in becoming the healthier person I want to be. Hold up for me a mirror of the new creation you see me becoming, for I need a companion at this table. "Lettuce pray!" Amen.

February 27

*God is our refuge and strength,
a very present help in trouble.*

—Psalm 46:1

Give me strength today to stand against temptation. Empower me with the faith that I can say no to things that don't add to my peace or happiness without guilt or regret. Give me, God, the courage to turn away from things that might bring fleeting pleasure, but may not be your will for me. I ask today in prayer for the strength to do what is right, what is just and what is fair, even if I am tempted to cheat, lie or take more than my fair share. Amen.

February 28

*After two days will he revive us:
in the third day he will raise us up,
and we shall live in his sight.*

—Hosea 6:2

February 29

And I will cleanse them
from all their iniquity,
whereby they have sinned against me;
and I will pardon all their iniquities,
whereby they have sinned,
and whereby they have transgressed
against me.

—*Jeremiah* 33:8

How can we put others' mistakes in
perspective? God not only forgives the
sin but understands the heart of the
sinner. We tiny mortals can try to do
the same! True forgiveness brings us
closer to God, which is the
greatest blessing.

March

March 1

O thou afflicted, tossed with tempest,
and not comforted,
behold, I will lay thy stones with fair colours,
and lay thy foundations with sapphires.

—Isaiah 54:11

O Lord God, this horrible disaster has really been
a blow to my family and me. It was so unexpected.
One day, everything is fine; the next day, everything
is gone. Our extended family, friends, and church all
want to help us, and we are truly grateful for their
generous compassion, but still we feel utterly defeat-
ed. A lifetime of hard work is wiped out, and now we
have to start over. Please help us, Lord, to be thankful
that we have our lives and each other,
and most importantly, that we
have you to take care of us.
Help us, we pray in Jesus'
precious name. Amen.

March 2

> *Thou wilt shew me the path of life:*
> *in thy presence* is *fulness of joy;*
> *at thy right hand* there are
> *pleasures for evermore.*
>
> —Psalm 16:11

Today, Lord, I've come into your presence again, just to be near you. Whether you have a new insight for me or just a reassurance of your care for me, I'm happy for the opportunity to commune with you right now. Help me stay close to you throughout the day, and please keep your song of joy alive in my heart, fueled by gratitude for all the goodness you bring into my life. You are the one who makes my life truly worthwhile. May I remain in step with you along this blessing-filled path of life.

March 3

Open thou mine eyes,
that I may behold wondrous things
out of thy law.

—*Psalm 119:18*

There was a time in my life when I tried to read your Word, and it just didn't mean that much to me because I didn't understand it. But Lord, the longer I've walked with you, the more precious, meaningful, and essential the scriptures have become to me. Thank you for giving me the comprehension to perceive your truth. Please continue to open my understanding to the teachings of your Spirit—the truths written in your Word—that I may walk even more closely with you.

March 4

*What is my strength,
that I should hope?
and what is mine end,
that I should prolong my life?*

—Job 6:11

Imagine having someone always beside you to help you navigate the choppy waters of life? Imagine being able to turn within and ask for strength, courage, love, care, or guidance whenever it is needed? The thing is, you do have someone exactly like this, even though you may have forgotten. You have God.

March 5

> *I have not hid thy righteousness*
> *within my heart;*
> *I have declared thy faithfulness*
> *and thy salvation:*
> *I have not concealed thy lovingkindness*
> *and thy truth from the great congregation.*
>
> —*Psalm 40:10*

Dear Lord, when I sense that you are opening an opportunity for me to talk to someone about you—whether it's a word about your saving grace, your faithfulness, or your constant love—help me to not be afraid to speak up. Help me treat those to whom I'm speaking with gentleness and respect as I share my faith in you. And for those who are looking for you, may my words help them find you.

March 6

All of what I call "my strengths" are from you, dear Lord. You are the source of all strength, and I am dependent on you each day for everything. I want to be a child who "shouts" and sings for joy because of you, O God, my strength and provider.

March 7

I understand that my sense of justice is not like yours, heavenly Father. Yours is perfect, while mine is limited and skewed, lopsided in favor of myself, and I never have all the illuminating facts and information to be able to judge exactly right where others are concerned. So I'm grateful, Lord, that you know precisely how to bring wickedness to light and to deal with it. And you know how to reward what is right and true and good. Help me live uprightly, truthfully, and honorably that I might be firmly established as one who walks in your ways, Lord.

March 8

*Behold, thou desirest truth
in the inward parts:
and in the hidden part thou shalt
make me to know wisdom.*

—Psalm 51:6

Truth may hurt initially when we learn it, just as a needle piercing an infected wound. But after all of the pent-up lies, pride, and pretense have been let out, there is a wonderful feeling of relief and freedom that quickly follows as we embrace the cleansing of God's loving truth.

March 9

My Lord, where are you? You seem far away lately. Am I doing something wrong? Should I be praying differently or more often? Have I mistreated some friend or relative? Is that why you're so distant? Do I have a bad attitude about something? I don't know. Please let me know what the problem is so I can fix it. I long to feel your presence close to me again. Life is hard enough on its own, but I can't imagine living without you. I need to know that you're right beside me. Are you here, Lord? Please reveal yourself to me.

March 10

Let my prayer be set forth
before thee *as incense;*
and the lifting up of my hands
as the evening sacrifice.
—*Psalm* 141:2

In ancient times the sweet smell of incense would rise from the Israelites' houses of worship. Today I ask you to accept the sweetness of my praises. I love you with all that I am. I devote myself to you. I honor and glorify you. I lift my heart to you, as well as my hands. Receive my praises and enjoy their aroma. They come from a sincere heart.

March 11

It takes great courage to heal, Lord, great energy to reach out from this darkness to touch the hem of your garment and ask for healing. Bless the brave voices telling nightmare tales of dreadful wounds to the gifted healers of this world. Together, sufferers and healers are binding up damaged parts and laying down burdens carried so long.

March 12

Yea, thou castest off fear,
and restrainest prayer before God.

—Job 15:4

God, I pray to you today for the healing that only you can bring. I long to be free from pain and suffering, to be whole again in body, mind, and spirit. Give to me the soothing balm of your tender, loving care that I might mount up on wings of eagles and fly with ease again. Amen.

March 13

Creating the universe. Making human beings. Speaking to Abraham and leading him. Parting the Red Sea. Giving the Law. Stopping the sun in its tracks. Burning Elijah's wet sacrifice. Taming Daniel's lions. Coming to earth as a baby . . . These are just some of the mighty deeds I praise you for, O Lord.

March 14

Loving Father, you know I don't mind
being alone at times, but when loneli-
ness sets in, there's a sense of isolation and sadness that overcomes
me. You made me to be a relational person, and yet sometimes
you allow me to experience a
famine of relationships in my
life. It's at these times that
I feel tremendous need
for company to soothe
the ache and fill the void.
Please be my oasis in these
times of drought. Be near me, and
remind me of your presence in
ways I can grasp and in ways that
comfort and console me. Thank you
for always being with me.

March 15

Thou compassest my path
and my lying down,
and art acquainted with all my ways.
for there is not a word in my tongue,
but, lo, O Lord, thou knowest it altogether.

—*Psalm 139:3-4*

God, shine your healing light down upon me today, for my path is filled with painful obstacles and my suffering fogs my vision. Clear the challenges from the road I must walk upon, or at least walk with me as I confront them. With you, I know I can endure anything. With you, I know I can make it through to the other side, where joy awaits. Amen.

March 16

> *Finally, my brethren, be strong in the Lord,
> and in the power of his might.
> Put on the whole armour of God,
> that ye may be able to stand
> against the wiles of the devil.*
>
> —Ephesians 6:10-11

God, I know you will never give us a burden to bear without giving us the grace to endure it, but some burdens just seem so heavy we find ourselves wondering if they can be survived. I ask that you send an abundant amount of strength and grace to all those who suffer so. Let them feel your presence in a very real way, Lord, for without you, they have no hope. I ask this in Jesus' name. Amen.

March 17

> *I taught Ephraim also to go,*
> *taking them by their arms;*
> *but they knew not that I healed them.*
>
> —Hosea 11:3

Lord, this healing process is sometimes slow, and I get discouraged and filled with doubt. Can I take this? Will I make it? Yet you always remind me of your powerful presence and assure me that where I am unable to go, you will go for me and what I am unable to do by myself, you will do for me. Thank you, Lord. Amen.

March 18

> For I will restore health unto thee,
> and I will heal thee of thy wounds,
> saith the Lord;
> because they called thee an Outcast, *saying*,
> This *is* Zion, whom no man seeketh after.
>
> —Jeremiah 30:17

Lord, bless all those today who need healing of any kind. Whether it be physical, emotional, or mental, bless them with your merciful grace and eternal love. Let each one know that they are special in your eyes and that, in the realm of spirit, there is only perfection, wholeness, and joy. Amen.

March 19

But be not thou far from me, O Lord:
O my strength, haste thee to help me.
—*Psalm 22:19*

When I feel my control slipping, Lord,
I know I only have to call on you for
encouragement, direction, and guidance to get your loving assistance.

March 20

And whatsoever ye shall ask in my name,
that will I do, that the Father
may be glorified in the Son.
If ye shall ask any thing in my name,
I will do *it*.

—John 14:13–14

March 21

Behold, the hour cometh,
yea, is now come,
that ye shall be scattered,
every man to his own,
and shall leave me alone:
and yet I am not alone,
because the Father is with me.

—John 16:32

March 22

Bless the soil beneath our feet, the sky overhead, and make us one with it. We are catching on, catching up with ourselves, creator God, and catching a whiff of the garbage we're burying ourselves beneath. Catching, too, a glimpse of the fading streams and trash-strewn seas we have long ignored. With your help, we can bind up and reclaim this poor old earth. We feel whispers of hope in the winds of changed hearts and minds, for we recall your promise to make all things new—even this earth we shall yet learn to tend. We are grateful for another chance.

March 23

> *Comfort ye, comfort ye my people,*
> *saith your God.*
>
> —Isaiah 40:1

Dear Lord, thank you for healing my heart and bringing joy and meaning back into my life. Thank you for the people who truly care for me. Help me be a soothing and joyful presence in their lives as well. Amen.

March 24

Let the thought that
He knows my need before I ask,
bring me, in great restfulness of faith,
to trust that He will give
what His child requires.

—Henry Altemus

Heavenly Father, please help me realize there are different forms of healing. There are moments when life doesn't seem to change and I have to look inside to find a place of acceptance. It is in this place where I am reminded that who I am is separate from the pain that invades my life. Please help me to turn my thoughts to you. Amen.

March 25

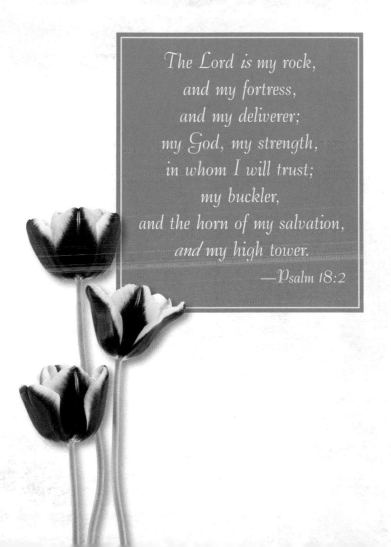

The Lord *is* my rock,
and my fortress,
and my deliverer;
my God, my strength,
in whom I will trust;
my buckler,
and the horn of my salvation,
and my high tower.

—*Psalm* 18:2

March 26

> But the God of all grace,
> who hath called us unto
> his eternal glory by Christ Jesus,
> after that ye have suffered a while,
> make you perfect, stablish,
> strengthen, settle you.
>
> —1 Peter 5:10

Her hands are so gentle and skilled, her mind so quick, her heart so filled with compassion. Bless her in all her duties, and in her free time, too. For she needs physical and spiritual refreshment these days, and you, Great Physician, are the one who can help her the best.

March 27

> *Be not wise in thine own eyes:*
> *fear the Lord, and depart from evil.*
> *It shall be health to thy navel,*
> *and marrow to thy bones.*
>
> —*Proverbs 3:7-8*

Dear God, hear my prayer. I am suffering and in need of your merciful blessings. Please take me into your arms. Give me the courage to keep going through difficult times and the fortitude to move beyond the outer illusions of pain and despair. Only you can heal me, God. In praise and thanks, Amen.

March 28

Heal me, O Lord, and I shall be healed;
save me, and I shall be saved:
for thou art my praise.

—Jeremiah 17:14

Is illness your will, Lord? I need answers, for I want you to help me heal. But if you send illness, how can I trust you to heal? Reassure me that you will work everything out eventually. And when that isn't possible, be with me as I suffer. Freed from fear I can get stronger as your healing energy flows through me, restoring me to my abundant life.

March 29

> *Fear thou not; for I am with thee:*
> *be not dismayed; for I am thy God:*
> *I will strengthen thee; yea, I will help thee;*
> *yea, I will uphold thee with the right hand*
> *of my righteousness.*
>
> — Isaiah 41:10

Lord, please be my strength. When I am scared, please make me brave. When I am unsteady, please bring your stability to me. I look to your power for an escape from the pain. I welcome your comfort.

March 30

Father, my willpower is no match for resisting the fears encroaching on my heart and mind. I can resolve in the morning to not be afraid, but unless I keep my eyes fixed steadily on you, fear creeps in the door or blasts through my resistances or catches me off guard. And you know how easily distracted I become when the day is underway. Oh, Father! I don't want to resist my fears with mere willpower. Help me abandon that strategy entirely and rely on you instead. Remind me again and again that trusting you means refusing to lean on my own understanding and strength; I need to choose instead to lean on yours. Amen.

March 31

I will bless the Lord,
who hath given me counsel:
my reins also instruct me
in the night seasons.

—Psalm 16:7

April

April 1

> *The Lord will strengthen him*
> *upon the bed of languishing:*
> *thou wilt make all his bed in his sickness.*
>
> —*Psalm* 41:3

Oh Lord, the pain is unrelenting today. Not even painkillers are helping. Please deliver me from my awful wretchedness! What do you want me to do in order for you to respond to my pleas? How do you want me to pray? Surely you can't bear to see me in so much agony? Oh Lord, display your love for me by ridding me of this piercing pain! My Lord, please forgive me for being presumptuous. The pain is so severe I can't think straight. I know that more than anything I need you beside me to sustain me. I know this pain is temporary and what awaits me is eternal joy in your heavenly kingdom.

April 2

Bless the Lord, O my soul,
and forget not all his benefits:
who forgiveth all thine iniquities;
who healeth all thy diseases;
who redeemeth thy life from destruction;
who crowneth thee with lovingkindness and
tender mercies.

—Psalm 103:2–4

April 3

This physical affliction, Lord, is like a snake wrapped tightly around my soul, squeezing the life out of me. It stares at me with cold, deathlike eyes, and it hisses at me with its snarling tongue and sharp fangs. I feel helpless and frozen in its grasp. Not only is the hurt intense, but I'm also gripped with fear that my suffering will become even worse. Lord, please deliver me from this ghastly serpent! I'm in need of immediate rescue, and I cry out for the help only you can bring to me. Help me, Lord! I pray in the name of my precious Savior, Jesus Christ. Amen.

April 4

Let us therefore come boldly
unto the throne of grace,
that we may obtain mercy,
and find grace to help in time of need.
—Hebrews 4:16

April 5

> *The sacrifices of God are a broken spirit:*
> *a broken and a contrite heart,*
> *O God, thou wilt not despise.*
>
> —*Psalm 51:17*

I come to you humbly, My Lord, well aware of my sins. I have done things to displease you, and I have avoided doing things you wanted me to do. I have not listened to your voice enough. Instead, I often go my own rebellious way. And I bow before you now in sorrow with a broken spirit and a contrite heart. Please forgive my sins. Jesus sacrificed himself as atonement for my sins, and I claim that sacrifice now. Wipe the record clean and restore our love, I pray.

April 6

Thou, O God,
didst send a plentiful rain,
whereby thou didst confirm
thine inheritance,
when it was weary.
Thy congregation
hath dwelt therein:
thou, O God,
hast prepared of
thy goodness
for the poor.
—Psalm 68:9–10

April 7

> *A wicked messenger falleth into mischief:*
> *but a faithful ambassador is health.*
>
> —*Proverbs 13:17*

Father God, we know that to receive the blessing of healing, the heart must be open. But when we are mad, we close off the heart as if it were a prison. Remind us that a heart that is shut cannot receive understanding, acceptance, and renewal. Even though we feel angry, we must keep the heart's door slightly ajar so your grace can enter and fill our darkness with the light of hope.

April 8

Great God, I thank you for the many times you have met my needs—not only material needs but emotional, relational, and spiritual needs as well. Sometimes with near-miracles, but usually in subtler ways, you work your wonders, and I have been blessed. I thank you for the care you've shown to me, and I ask you to help me care for others. Give me eyes to see the needs around me and the strength to do what I can to show your love.

April 9

> *He will swallow up death in victory;*
> *and the Lord God will wipe away tears*
> *from off all faces;*
> *and the rebuke of his people*
> *shall he take away from off all the earth:*
> *for the Lord hath spoken it.*
>
> — *Isaiah 25:8*

May your thoughts focus much more upon what you have than what you lack in this trying time. May your heart lay hold of present realities rather than future possibilities. For this moment—the now—is in front of us. Whether we are sick or healthy, this juncture in time is the place we share. Let us be blessed in this moment, safe in our knowledge of God's plan for us. Let us simply be in God's presence, just for this moment.

April 10

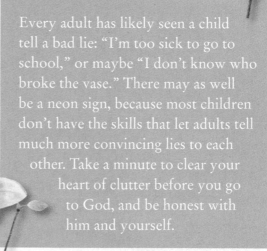

Every adult has likely seen a child
tell a bad lie: "I'm too sick to go to
school," or maybe "I don't know who
broke the vase." There may as well
be a neon sign, because most children
don't have the skills that let adults tell
much more convincing lies to each
other. Take a minute to clear your
heart of clutter before you go
to God, and be honest with
him and yourself.

April 11

Restore unto me the joy of thy salvation;
and uphold me with thy free spirit.

—Psalm 51:12

I come to you with a tired soul.
My will seems weak; my faith feels old.
I've said the words, the prayers I've prayed;
Good deeds I've done; I've seldom strayed.
My interaction with you, Lord,
Is fine—but now I'm getting bored.
I trust you still for daily bread,
Just lately I've been playing dead.
But wait! Before the break of day
My tombstone slowly rolls away!
The Lord of life stands tall and strong.
I think I hear a victory song.
The risen Christ is raised indeed,
And after that, he raises me.
Salvation's joy has been restored.
Sing praises to our living Lord!

April 12

*As well the singers as the players
on instruments shall be there:
all my springs are in thee.*

—Psalm 87:7

Dear Lord, the psalmist spoke about springs of water, and maybe the idea was that the creativity of these artists was springing up from the depths of their relationship with you. That makes me think about the ways I display my own creativity and how it all originates with you. But it's also fun to imagine dancers "springing" and leaping with divine joy. Do I have an extra "spring in my step" because I know you? I also find myself  in the season of spring, with new life sprouting all around me. Every day with you is like springtime, full of life and growth. Lord, in these ways I celebrate you, singing with the psalmist, "All my springs are in you."

April 13

*And Jesus went forth,
and saw a great multitude,
and was moved with compassion toward them,
and he healed their sick.*

—Matthew 14:14

Lord, you do not leave us to suffer alone. You are with us in pain, in sickness, and in our worst moments. Thank you for your comfort and healing power. Thank you for getting us through when our bodies fail, when our health falters, and when we need you most of all. Amen.

April 14

*Notwithstanding the Lord
stood with me,
and strengthened me;
that by me the preaching
might be fully known,
and that all the Gentiles might hear:
and I was delivered
out of the mouth of the lion.*

—2 Timothy 4:17

There's a place of renewal and happiness within you. All you need to do to reach it is withdraw your attention from the outside world and focus on the strength and the energy inside yourself.

April 15

> *I have seen his ways, and will heal him:*
> *I will lead him also,*
> *and restore comforts unto him*
> *and to his mourners.*
>
> —Isaiah 57:18

Help me recover from this ambush of illness, Great Physician, and the worry it brings. Reassure my fearful heart that my sickness was never intended; it just happened. Bodies break down, parts age, and minds weary. Your assurance gives me strength to hang on.

April 16

Jesus healed many without resorting to miracles and seems to have resorted to the miraculous only to convince his hearers of his authority in divine matters. In some cases, as the woman who touched his garment, he claimed nothing for himself, but told her that her own faith had served her.

—Russell H. Conwell

April 17

*I will go into thy house
with burnt offerings:
I will pay thee my vows,
which my lips have uttered,
and my mouth hath spoken,
when I was in trouble.*
—*Psalm 66:13-14*

April 18

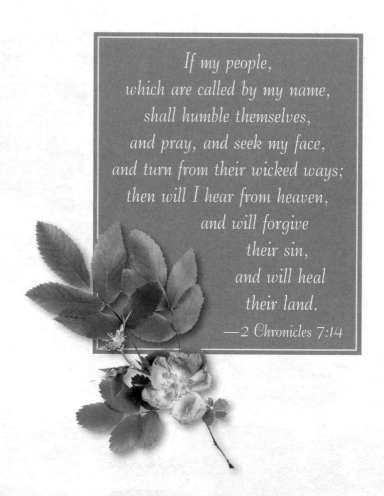

If my people,
which are called by my name,
shall humble themselves,
and pray, and seek my face,
and turn from their wicked ways;
then will I hear from heaven,
and will forgive
their sin,
and will heal
their land.

—2 Chronicles 7:14

April 19

*He sent his word, and healed them,
and delivered them from their destructions.*

—*Psalm 107:20*

Illness makes our moods like a children's wind-up
toy, crazily up one minute, flat down the next; we
cry and laugh, we worry and celebrate! Getting well
is hard, complicated work. May God lead us into full
recovery, but carefully—we're still a bit unpredictable.

April 20

When we pray for healing, we pray for wholeness. Our prayers may be answered even if we don't receive exactly what we thought we asked for: The terminally ill person may be healed, yet not live; the chronically pained may still have physical suffering, yet their healing may mean they have been given an inner peace with which the physical problems are faced.

April 21

> *Behold, happy is the man*
> *whom God correcteth:*
> *therefore despise not thou*
> *the chastening of the Almighty:*
> *for he maketh sore, and bindeth up:*
> *he woundeth, and his hands make whole.*
>
> —Job 5:17-18

God, we know that pain has produced some wisdom in our lives, but it has also created cynicism and fear. People turn on us, reject us, hurt us, and none of us wants to play the fool more than once, so we're tempted to close off our hearts to people and to you. But relationships that bring meaning and joy require vulnerability. Help us trust you to be our truest friend and to lead us to the kind of community that will bring healing rather than destruction.

April 22

*Is not Jesus Christ the same yesterday,
today, and forever?
Why should we wonder, therefore,
at his healing touch in this age?
According to your faith be it unto you.*

—Rosalind Goforth

Our hearts are bruised, Father, black and blue from life's pounding. Swollen and sore from hurts real and imagined. We need a soothing balm to ease our discomfort. Please send into our lives those who have healing hands and helping hearts, those who would salve our pain by word and deed.

April 23

Lord, it is difficult to talk about death with my children. When friends or relatives die, my children need to know that death is a natural part of life; that this earthly life is not all there is; that we will all meet again in heaven. Yet the earthly loss is painful. My children need to know that you are with them. Help me to find the words that will point them to you, Lord—words that will glorify you, words that will soothe and take away my children's fears.

April 24

How much our Christianity suffers from this, that it is confined to certain times and places. A man who seeks to pray earnestly in the church or in the closet, spends the greater part of the week or the day in a spirit entirely at variance with that in which he prayed. His worship was the work of a fixed place or hour, not of his whole being.

—Henry Altemus

April 25

We know how often a man may be suffering from a disease without knowing it. What he counts a slight ailment turns out to be a dangerous complaint. Do not let us be too sure that we are not, to a large extent, still living "under the law," while considering ourselves to be living wholly "under grace."

—Rev. Andrew Murray

April 26

Dear God, help us start anew. Teach us how to heal
by learning new ways to live. Amen.

April 27

> *Then shall thy light break forth as the morning,*
> *and thine health shall spring forth speedily:*
> *and thy righteousness shall go before thee;*
> *the glory of the Lord shall be thy rereward.*
>
> —*Isaiah 58:8*

When illness strikes, the effects go beyond the physical suffering. Fear, despair, and terrible isolation arise as the illness prolongs itself. It feels natural to lash out at your failing body, medicine that does not help, and even at the God who allowed this terrible thing to happen to you. The fate of the patient's loved ones can be equally painful, as they stand by feeling helpless to be of any real assistance. Yet, be assured that the Lord is there among you.

April 28

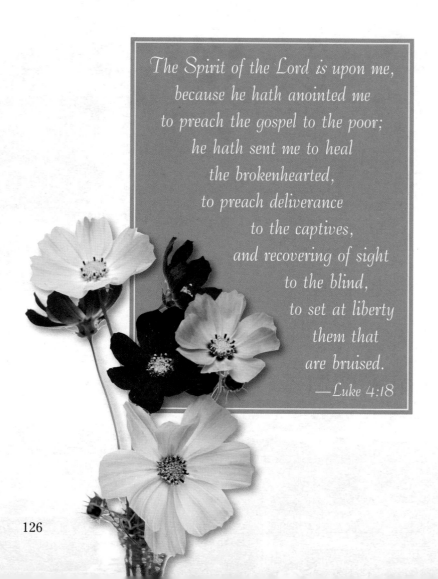

The Spirit of the Lord *is* upon me,
because he hath anointed me
to preach the gospel to the poor;
he hath sent me to heal
the brokenhearted,
to preach deliverance
to the captives,
and recovering of sight
to the blind,
to set at liberty
them that
are bruised.

—Luke 4:18

April 29

When joy and laughter vanish
Into illness and despair,
I remind myself that with God's help
You can get there from here.
So let not doubt and fear take seed
And grow into a tree,
But let God's healing make me whole
And love take root in me.

April 30

Bring your cool caress to the foreheads of those suffering fever. By your spirit, lift the spirits of the bedridden and give comfort to those in pain. Strengthen all entrusted with the care of the infirm today, and give them renewed energy for their tasks. And remind us all that heaven awaits—where we will all be whole and healthy before you, brothers and sisters forever.

May

May 1

> *And Cornelius said, Four days ago I was fasting until this hour; and at the ninth hour I prayed in my house, and, behold, a man stood before me in bright clothing, and said, Cornelius, thy prayer is heard, and thine alms are had in remembrance in the sight of God.*
>
> —Acts 10:30–31

Going through a difficult time alone feels like trying to find your way through a pitch-black room. The moment you reach out to another, a light appears that guides you to the other side, where the door to healing awaits.

May 2

God, the blessed feeling of being at home in your loving presence is like nothing else. The joy I feel when I know I never walk alone is the greatest of gifts, and when I look around at the wonderful people you have chosen to walk with me through life —my family and my friends—I truly know that I am loved. Thank you, God, for these miracles, these blessings, far too numerous to count. And to think I never have to look too far from home to find them is the best miracle of all.

May 3

May you know that a wisdom and a love transcend the things you will see and touch today. Walk in this light each step of the way. Never forget that there is more to this existence than the material side of things. And be blessed when you suddenly become aware of it: in the smile of a child, in the recognition of your own soul's existence, in the dread of death, and in the longing for immortality.

May 4

God, I couldn't help noticing all the love-
liness you placed in the world today! This
morning I saw a sunrise that made my
heart beat faster. I watched a father gently
help his child across a busy parking lot; his
tenderness was much like yours. I spied
an elderly couple sitting on a bench. As
the man told jokes, their laughter lifted
my spirits. Later, I talked with a friend
who aids needy families; her compassion
inspired me. Thank you, Lord, for
everything that is beautiful and
good in the world.

May 5

The surge of adrenaline as we look over our shoulders to see who's gaining on us is as natural as breathing, Lord, and we pick up the pace to keep ahead. Competition is exhilarating, and we welcome its challenges. Yet, competition out of control creates bare-knuckle conflict within us, and we are shocked at the lengths to which we will go to win. We must look ahead to you, not backward to those we're "besting."

May 6

> *Hatred stirreth up strifes:*
> *but love covereth all sins.*
>
> —Proverbs 10:12

Bless this gathering of what, at first glance, looks like mismatched parts, encircling God, for we want to become a family. Guide us as we step closer to one another, but not so close as to crowd. Heal wounds from past events that made this union possible. Bless the children with the courage to try new relatives, new traditions, new homes. Step closer, loving God, and lead us.

May 7

> I have been young, and *now* am old;
> yet have I not seen the righteous forsaken,
> nor his seed begging bread.
>
> —Psalm 37:25

About devotional feelings, about religious observances, however excellent and blessed, we may deceive ourselves; for we may put them in the place of sanctification, of righteousness and true holiness. About justice and honesty we cannot deceive ourselves; for they are sanctification itself, righteousness itself, true holiness itself, the very likeness of God, and the very grace of God.

—Charles Kingsley

Sometimes your
medicine bottle has on it,
"shake well before using."
That is what God has to do
with some of His people.
He has to shake them well
before they are ever usable.

—Vance Havner

May 9

> *I will lift up mine eyes unto the hills,*
> *from whence cometh my help.*
> *My help cometh from the Lord,*
> *which made heaven and earth.*
>
> —Psalm 121:1–2

May 10

Heavenly Father, you are great! I am truly grateful for your salvation, and as I continually seek you, I rejoice in everything you reveal to me about yourself. I am, indeed, glad in you today. I feel blessed and deeply honored to be here with you, the God of the universe. When I try to think about it, it's a reality that's hard to wrap my mind around, and yet it's true. May I continually be in awe of your greatness and be full of delight when I reflect on who you are and how you have saved me.

May 11

Behold, God is mine helper:
the Lord is with them that uphold my soul.

—*Psalm* 54:4

When things go wrong in my life, dear Lord, help me
live out this declaration. May I entrust to you all that
pertains to my life, even my life itself: from broken
appliances to broken bones and to broken promises—
every form of fragmentation, frustration, and pain
that life in this fallen world can dish out. May I seek
and know you as my helper, the upholder of my life.

May 12

Precious Lord, your Word reveals that patience is the fruit of a life lived in step with your Holy Spirit. Therefore, I ask that, instead of my trying to be patient through self effort or beating myself up for my lack of patience, you would help me focus on being led by your Spirit in all circumstances, allowing your Spirit to guide me, speak into my life, and live through me at each juncture where patience is required. As I focus on following your lead, I know my life will begin to bear that good fruit of patient waiting and living.

May 13

*I have made the earth,
the man and the beast
that are upon the ground,
by my great power
and by my outstretched arm,
and have given it unto
whom it seemed meet unto me.*

—Jeremiah 27:5

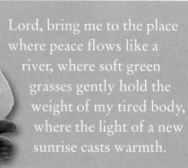

Lord, bring me to the place where peace flows like a river, where soft green grasses gently hold the weight of my tired body, where the light of a new sunrise casts warmth.

May 14

There are many events in our lives over which we have no control. However, we do have a choice either to endure trying times and press on or to give up. The secret of survival, whether or not we question God's presence or his ability to help us, is remembering that our hope is in the fairness, goodness, and justice of God. When we put our trust in the character of a God who cannot fail us, we will remain faithful. Our trust and faithfulness produce the endurance that sees us through the "tough stuff" we all face in this life.

May 15

> For this cause we also, since the day
> we heard it, do not cease to pray for you,
> and to desire that ye might be filled
> with the knowledge of his will in all wisdom
> and spiritual understanding.
>
> —Colossians 1:9

Paul's love and fellowship shines through in his epistles where he, like Christians ever since, reaches out to support people who have recently heard the good news. When we struggle, ache, and suffer, our fellows surround us and help us to heal. Relationships and community can strengthen the fortress of faith more than almost anything else.

May 16

Behold, I will bring it health and cure,
and I will cure them, and will reveal
unto them the abundance of peace and truth.

—Jeremiah 33:6

Inner peace and calm are vital to health. Chronic stress weakens our immune systems and impairs our bodies and minds. When spiritual life seeks to replace illness and doubt with "peace and truth," our minds and bodies can thrive.

May 17

*But now, O Lord, thou art our father;
we are the clay, and thou our potter;
and we all are the work of thy hand.*

—Isaiah 64:8

Have you worked with clay? It's flexible, strong, and almost impossible to ruin. God is the potter, but we, the clay, must hold our shape and endure. If we're marred, the flaws can be smoothed.

May 18

I the Lord do keep it;
I will water it every moment:
lest any hurt it, I will keep it night and day.

—Isaiah 27:3

To nurture is a constant job. God's ever-present attention gives us the tools we need but we must choose to take those tools and grow toward the sun of his love.

May 19

> Is any sick among you?
> let him call for the elders of the church;
> and let them pray over him,
> anointing him with oil
> in the name of the Lord.
>
> —James 5:14

Any illness is a shame, especially if a child is sick. We trust in the medicine and science God has made possible, but prayer shows both God and our loved ones how invested we are.

May 20

*If the spirit of the ruler rise up against thee,
leave not thy place;
for yielding pacifieth great offences.*

—*Ecclesiastes 10:4*

Lord, we expect to learn that "life isn't fair," but when it hurts the most is when our loved ones experience misfortune or injustice. Sometimes we try to interfere and cushion the fall but they resist and must learn for themselves in their own time. Help me to yield to your will even when I think I see the clearest path for them, and help me to welcome them back with forgiving and open arms.

May 21

Blessed is the person who has steadfast and unmoving faith when everything is going wrong. That's when faith is most needed. If a person can look beyond the illusion of negative appearances and believe in a higher power at work, faith will move mountains and bring positive solutions.

May 22

O my Lord! Strengthen my faith
so in the Father's tender love and kindness,
that as often as I feel sinful or troubled,
the first instinctive thought may be to go
where I know the Father waits me,
and where prayer never can go unblessed.
— *Henry Altemus*

May 23

> *Help me, O Lord my God:*
> *O save me according to thy mercy:*
> *that they may know that this is thy hand;*
> *that thou, Lord, hast done it.*
>
> —*Psalm* 109:26–27

Some people say adult life is like high school repeated, with all the cliques, scheming, and backstabbing you could ask for. But our relationship with God should make us bigger and better. Living well is the best payback, as they say.

May 24

Be still, and know that I am God:
I will be exalted among the heathen,
I will be exalted in the earth.
—Psalm 46:10

At times when stillness is not part of
my outer world, Lord, I need more than
ever to answer your call to quiet my
heart and mind before you. I thank you
that when I do stop to regain perspective, remembering that you are God,
everything else finds its proper place
in light of who you are. I have come to
be still right now and to exalt you as
God in my life. I thank you that I can
place myself under your sov-
ereignty and find peace in
your safety, provi-
sion, and love.

May 25

*And ye shall seek me, and find me,
when ye shall search for me
with all your heart.*

—*Jeremiah* 29:13

Traumatic events leave a void in our souls that only a closer relationship with God can fill. By asking God to help us through hard times, we truly come to understand that we are never alone and that sadness is only a precursor to joy and pain a precursor to healing.

May 26

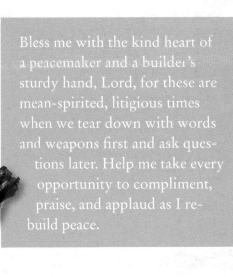

But without faith *it is* impossible to please *him:* for he that cometh to God must believe that he is, and *that* he is a rewarder of them that diligently seek him.

—Hebrews 11:6

Bless me with the kind heart of a peacemaker and a builder's sturdy hand, Lord, for these are mean-spirited, litigious times when we tear down with words and weapons first and ask questions later. Help me take every opportunity to compliment, praise, and applaud as I rebuild peace.

May 27

> *God be merciful unto us, and bless us;*
> *and cause his face to shine upon us.*
>
> —*Psalm 67:1*

When your blessings flow into my life, dear Lord, it certainly feels like situational sunshine, as if you are looking upon my life with a megawatt smile. Help me remember your blessings and recount them often so that I do not forget that I have been and always am sustained solely by your grace. In Jesus' name, I pray. Amen.

May 28

Deliver me, O my God,
out of the hand of the wicked,
out of the hand of the unrighteous
and cruel man.

—Psalm 71:4

Jesus, you know what it is to be lied about, unjustly condemned, and cruelly tortured and killed at the hands of wicked people. I ask that you would hear my cry for help to be set free from the evil schemes of those who would try to harm me without cause. I look to you alone for my defense. Please rescue me! In your name, I pray. Amen.

May 29

There is much I have done—or failed to do—that I would change. But these are irretrievable realities, and yet, they are not unredeemable. Each wrong that I bring to you and confess, you readily forgive and begin the process of redemption, of bringing some good out of the aftermath of my downfall. I'm deeply grateful for these miracles, but I pray that you would cause me to grow wiser from my mistakes and more faithful so I can walk in your righteousness.

May 30

All-powerful Lord, sometimes my prayer life seems like a list of needs or a litany of superficial thoughts. My heart isn't always in it. And when I think about how a human relationship would fare if there was just cognitive communication with no heart-level interaction, I see my deep need to engage my heart in our relationship. Help me as I seek to open up to you more and more in the days ahead.

May 31

He hath filled the hungry with good things;
and the rich he hath sent empty away.

—Luke 1:53

Prayer had been her solace and strength
during all these days and nights,
and now with passionate entreaty
she beseeched God for guidance and help
in the struggle that was to come.
When she rose from her knees her fear
had vanished, and she was tranquil
and confident. For God was good,
and He was leading her,
and that was perfect happiness.

— William Pringle Livingstone

June

June 1

Lord, I just want to tell you how much I love you, how grateful I am that you have taken me into your care. Ever since I've entrusted myself to you, you've kept me from becoming entangled in the kinds of things that would bring me to ruin. You fill my heart and mind with peace as I stay close to you. It's a miracle of your grace that I am standing tall today, lifting my praise to you from a heart full of love.

June 2

We live in a society that knows nothing of delayed gratification; we often get caught up in the expectation that everything we need from you and ask of you will happen immediately. But we know from experience that your timing is always perfect, Lord. We are blessed and privileged to have time for reflection and growth.

June 3

Seeking courage, Lord, I bundle my fears and place them in your hands. Too heavy for me, too weighty even to ponder in this moment, such shadowy terrors shrink to size in my mind and—how wonderful!—wither to nothing in your grasp.

June 4

Have not I commanded thee?
Be strong and of a good courage;
be not afraid, neither be thou dismayed:
for the Lord thy God is
with thee whithersoever thou goest.

—Joshua 1:9

Lord, you're never missing in action—
you're with me all the time, everywhere,
without fail. Please keep this knowledge
in the forefront of my mind today so
I'll be encouraged and emboldened
to move through each challenge
without feeling intimidated,
fearful, or ashamed. In
your name, I pray.

June 5

> *Now the Lord is that Spirit:*
> *and where the Spirit of the Lord is,*
> *there is liberty.*
>
> *—2 Corinthians 3:17*

Lord, how blessed we are to live in a country where we are free to worship as we please. Help us to never take such freedom for granted. Today we ask you to bless any believers who are being persecuted for living out their faith. Draw especially near to them, Lord. Surround them with your mighty army of angels.

June 6

> *Then he answered and spake unto me, saying,*
> *This is the word of the Lord unto Zerubbabel,*
> *saying, Not by might, nor by power,*
> *but by my spirit, saith the Lord of hosts.*
>
> —Zechariah 4:6

Lord, thank you for being a part of my work today. I can always tell when a thought or an idea comes from you because it's just too perfect to have been my own! That you care enough to be involved in my work is a precious gift to me, Lord—one I would never want to be without.

June 7

Now our Lord Jesus Christ himself,
and God, even our Father,
which hath loved us,
and hath given *us* everlasting consolation
and good hope through grace,
comfort your hearts,
and stablish you
in every good word
and work.
—2 Thessalonians 2:16–17

June 8

Two *are* better than one;
because they have a good reward
for their labour. For if they fall,
the one will lift up his fellow:
but woe to him *that is* alone
when he falleth; for he *hath*
not another to help him up.

—Ecclesiastes 4:9–10

Lord, so many times when I've been down,
time with a good friend has lifted me up
again and helped me to face my circumstances with a better attitude. Sometimes that
friend is my best friend—my husband—but
other times it's one of my precious female
friends who seems to intuitively know the
precise advice I need. Thank you, Lord, for
dear friends. May I be such a friend to others.

June 9

And to love him with all the heart, and with all the understanding, and with all the soul, and with all the strength, and to love his neighbour as himself, is more than all whole burnt offerings and sacrifices.

—Mark 12:33

Lord, I often pray for others when I need to pray with others. Show me the power of shared prayer as I meet with others in your name and in your presence. Amen.

June 10

Too often, Lord, I make my own plans and forget about yours. I think I know what's best for me, and I set out my goals accordingly. But now I see that this isn't just ungodly, it's not smart. What do I know, compared to you? Do I really expect that I can make wise decisions independent from you? My creator, you made me! You know how I function best! Besides that, you know the rest of the world as well, and what effect I can have on it. So, Lord, right here and now, I acknowledge you. Be my guide through life. Make my paths straight.

June 11

> *Judge not, and ye shall not be judged:*
> *condemn not, and ye shall not be condemned:*
> *forgive, and ye shall be forgiven.*
>
> —*Luke 6:37*

Why is it often the people closest to us that hurt us the most? Today I ask for the strength to deal with difficult people in the way you would want me to. Today I ask for the ability to find it in my heart to forgive them their trespasses, as I would hope they'd forgive mine. Today I ask for enough love to look beyond their problems and see them as you see them, as human beings deserving of love and care, even if I have to do it from a distance. Help me to forgive and move on, God. Amen.

June 12

> For who is God, save the Lord?
> and who is a rock, save our God?
> God is my strength and power:
> and he maketh my way perfect.
> He maketh my feet like hinds' feet:
> and setteth me upon my high places.
>
> —2 Samuel 22:32–34

Trying to tackle life without God is like making your way alone through a dense jungle filled with all sorts of perils. It is rough going—discouraging, disheartening, and often disastrous. On the other hand, the life of faith is one of being led on a well-kept path. Even though trouble may come along, it cannot overwhelm us because the Lord strengthens and guards our souls when we call on him for help.

June 13

> *Whatever enlarges hope will*
> *also exalt courage.*
> —*Samuel Johnson*

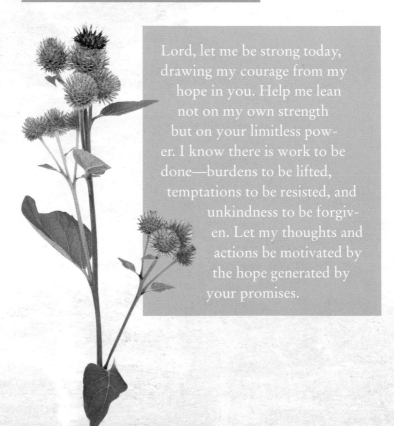

Lord, let me be strong today, drawing my courage from my hope in you. Help me lean not on my own strength but on your limitless power. I know there is work to be done—burdens to be lifted, temptations to be resisted, and unkindness to be forgiven. Let my thoughts and actions be motivated by the hope generated by your promises.

June 14

Blessed is the man that walketh not in the counsel of the ungodly, nor standeth in the way of sinners, nor sitteth in the seat of the scornful.

—*Psalm 1:1*

Kindness, compassion, and courtesy are contagious. Be true to your faith and values in your works. Wave a car ahead of you in traffic. Ask the supermarket checker about her day. Run errands for a sick friend. The language of an open and loving heart is heard in the quietest, most simple gestures.

June 15

> *And call upon me in the day of trouble:*
> *I will deliver thee, and thou shalt glorify me.*
> —*Psalms 50:15*

We think of God's mercy in a personal way—that he is merciful to us flawed human believers—but his mercy shines brightly each time he asks his people to spread the good word. With each new believer, God's love multiplies.

June 16

John Donne famously used the metaphor of God as fire and wrote that God can "break, blow, burn, and make me new." We are torn down and built back up by the fire, and, like pottery, we are stronger for it.

June 17

God, you are my rock and foundation. When the
storms of life rage around me, I know that I can seek
warmth and security in your loving grace. You are a
beacon guiding me through the thick fog of fear and
confusion to the safe comfort of the shore. Steady
and true are your love and your strength. Steadfast
and secure am I in the light of your changeless and
timeless presence that permeates the darkest of nights.

June 18

*Do all things without murmurings
and disputings: that ye may be blameless
and harmless, the sons of God,
without rebuke, in the midst of a crooked
and perverse nation, among whom ye shine
as lights in the world.*

—*Philippians 2:14–15*

Once the kids arrive, romance gets nudged aside by the carpool, and candlelit dinners happen only when the power is out. Which, we fear, God of love, could happen to us, the couple who were lovebirds once upon a time. Help us retrieve the "us" that supports the family, for we are a union blessed by you. As we cope with a full house now, remind us of empty nests ahead, a love-nest time just for us. Remind us to take a minute for ourselves amidst the loving chaos of family life.

June 19

My Lord, thank you for being generous with your gifts rather than giving them to only a select few. In fact, you make receiving them as simple as just asking. You never cease to amaze me with your generosity, Lord. I'm deeply grateful.

June 20

Both riches and honour *come* of thee,
and thou reignest over all;
and in thine hand *is* power and might;
and in thine hand *it is* to make great,
and to give strength unto all.

—1 Chronicles 29:12

Lord, today I pray for all struggling parents. Give them strength to hold fast to what they know is right even in the face of conflicting opinions and advice that is well meaning but off the mark nonetheless. You alone can supply the peace of mind they need to get through the toughest of times. Stay close to them, Lord, and amaze them with your works!

June 21

Be perfect, be of good comfort,
be of one mind, live in peace;
and the God of love
and peace shall be with you.

—*2 Corinthians 13:11*

It sometimes takes a tragic event to open our eyes to the blessings that surround us, to show us the joy in life's simple moments. Our family, friends, our neighbors, and our communities suddenly become havens of love, support, and comfort in the midst of tragedy. Wise is the person who can see the magic and wonder in simple things without having to suffer a great loss or disaster.

June 22

*But when he saw the multitudes,
he was moved with compassion on them,
because they fainted,
and were scattered abroad,
as sheep having no shepherd.*

—Matthew 9:36

Lord, you give me your compassion today.
When I look at the people around me, help
me to see them through your eyes. I know
you love us all equally, Lord. And you love
us completely and unconditionally. May I
compassionately reach out to others in your
name today.

June 23

Why does it seem impossible to wait patiently and graciously for an overdue phone call or long-expected letter, for an ailing loved one to get better? Is there a special ingredient to speed the passage of time and relieve my burdens? Lord, please teach me to wait patiently and trust in you.

June 24

We've had a falling out, Father. My friend and I are at odds, and I am frustrated with how unreasonable things have become. I know I need to own my part in what has transpired, but my pride is getting in the way. What if I'm the only one to apologize, especially when I feel I have the smaller part to confess in what went wrong? What if things are never truly addressed or forgiven on both sides? I don't want there to be a rift, but I also don't want to move forward under false pretenses. I need your wisdom, Father. That's why I'm here. Help me put my pride aside and listen to your heart in this matter.

June 25

*And, being assembled together with them,
commanded them that they should not depart
from Jerusalem, but wait for the promise
of the Father, which, saith he,
ye have heard of me.*

—Acts 1:4

After the most remarkable miracle of all, Jesus Christ
tells the apostles that they still must be patient. In the
meantime, they must be fueled by the Holy Spirit
and spread the word of God. They can't guess or
anticipate God's timeline.

June 26

Spending time in your Word, Lord God, as well as out in your creation, begins to push back the darkness that's been shrouding my soul. The light you bring is gentle, like the dawn gathering strength on the eastern horizon. Thank you for being so kind to me. Thank you for not giving up on me. I could not have made it through this time without you. You showed me how to care for a hurting soul, and now I know how to love others who are hurting. Thank you. Bless you, Father. Amen.

June 27

> *He maketh my feet like hinds' feet,*
> *and setteth me upon my high places.*
>
> —*Psalm 18:33*

My Lord, how easy it is to slip and fall. One minute I'm riding high, enjoying the blessings of life, and suddenly I crash to earth. Sometimes my own pride does me in. Sometimes I forget about you, Lord. Sometimes, like Peter walking on the sea, I pay more attention to the wind and waves than to you. Is there a way to stay up there in those "mountaintop experiences"? But it's not really the "experience" I want to hold onto, it's you. Please stay close to me, Lord, whether I'm feeling high or low. In the heights and in the depths, you are the one I cling to.

June 28

Are you here, Lord? I've never felt lonelier than I do
in this illness. When I despair, I repeat a child's prayer
or familiar verse and feel soothed to connect with
you. The act of praying reminds me of your presence
in both sickness and health. Please help me to hold
my head high so I may always feel the light of your
love on my face, even in my darkest times.

June 29

*Be not far from me; for trouble is near;
for there is none to help.*

—Psalm 22:11

Oh, Lord. With you, I learn that my past
troubles can trouble me no more. With you,
dear Lord, I am suddenly free.

June 30

July

July 1

> *God is a Spirit: and they that worship him must worship him in spirit and in truth.*
>
> —John 4:24

One phrase that has popped up in the Christian music market recently is "extreme worship." It seems that everything in our culture is moving toward some kind of extreme version of itself. We have extreme sports, extreme home improvement shows . . . and now extreme worship. But what God is looking for is not found in our form—it's found in the essence of our worship. It's not something anyone can readily identify by the appearance of a worshipper—it's something only God can see when he looks in our hearts.

July 2

The world can be a scary place, heavenly Father .With global warming, disease, and economic uncertainty, there's not much we can count on anymore. Except you. Fill me with faith. Help me trust you for true security. Let my life radiate with confidence in your love and power.

July 3

Lord, thou hast heard
the desire of the humble:
thou wilt prepare their heart,
thou wilt cause thine
ear to hear:
to judge the fatherless and
the oppressed,
that the man of the earth
may no more oppress.

—Psalm 10:17–18

July 4

The Lord is my light and my salvation;
whom shall I fear?
the Lord is the strength of my life;
of whom shall I be afraid?

—*Psalm 27:1*

This psalm asks a rhetorical question, Lord, but I will answer it anyway: No one! I need fear no one with you leading the way in my life. Search my heart, Lord. Help me to not compromise my faith in any way. As you go before me, help me stand strong in the light of your salvation and not give an inch of ground to fear.

July 5

Climate breakdown has been over the news in recent years, supreme Lord, and I admit it affects me too. I find myself worrying about this world, but I'm especially anxious about the well-being of my loved ones. It's not just our ecosystem's breakdown, Lord, but health care, inequality, and debt. What's ahead for us? What will the future bring? Grace. Healing. Your loving touch. Thank you, Lord, for the surety of your active presence.

July 6

*The Lord looked down from heaven
upon the children of men,
to see if there were any that
did understand, and seek God.*
—*Psalm 14:2*

Seeking God and his kingdom above
all else is the wisest investment we will
ever make in this life.

July 7

*And I will make of thee a great nation,
and I will bless thee,
and make thy name great;
and thou shalt be a blessing:
and I will bless them that bless thee,
and curse him that curseth thee:
and in thee shall all families
of the earth be blessed.*

—Genesis 12:2–3

Lord, the only blessing I ask for these days
is to restore my body and mind to wellness.
When I am healthy and strong, everything
else seems easier and I have the fortitude to
handle challenges that come my way. Bless
me with good health and vitality,
and help me treat my body right
and avoid stress when I can.

July 8

Hitherto have ye asked nothing in my name:
ask, and ye shall receive,
that your joy may be full.

—John 16:24

July 9

The prayer for this day is a commitment to be glad in you and to let that gladness overflow into song. I pray now for a renewed steadfastness of heart that will continue to pursue the practice of praise. Let today be a day of song, of singing your praises because you are faithful and good to me.

July 10

None but God can satisfy
the longing of
the immortal soul;
as the heart was made
for Him,
He only can fill it.

—Richard Trench

July 11

He maketh me to lie down in green pastures:
he leadeth me beside the still waters.
He restoreth my soul:
he leadeth me in the paths of righteousness
for his name's sake.

—Psalm 23:2–3

July 12

Delight thyself also in the Lord;
and he shall give thee
the desires of thine heart.
—Psalm 37:4

July 13

*He is wise in heart,
and mighty in strength:
who hath hardened himself
against him,
and hath prospered?*

—Job 9:4

*God's might to direct me.
God's power to protect me.
God's wisdom for my learning.
God's eye for my discerning.
God's ear for my hearing.
God's word for my clearing.*

—St. Patrick

July 14

Shew me thy ways,
O Lord; teach me thy paths.

—Psalm 25:4

When my way is drear,
precious Lord, linger near.
When the day is almost gone,
Hear my cry, hear my call,
Hold my hand, lest I fall,
Precious Lord, take my hand, lead me home.

July 15

The Lord hath spoken peace to my soul,
He hath blessed me abundantly,
Hath pardoned my sins;
He hath shown me great mercy
and saved me by his love.
I will sing of his goodness and mercy while I live,
And ever, forever will praise his holy name.
O how sweet to trust in God,
And to know your sins forgiven,
To believe his
precious word,
And be guided
by his love.
Therefore goodness
and mercy,
Shall follow me all the
days of my life. Amen.

July 16

If ye forsake the Lord,
and serve strange gods,
then he will turn and do you hurt,
and consume you,
after that he hath done you good.

—Joshua 24:20

God, when things go wrong, we usually blame you first. Forgive us for even considering that you would deliberately hurt one of your very own children. What could you possibly have to gain? Thank you for your presence, and please forgive our many sins.

July 17

I look around at my neighbors, dear Lord, and I wonder where they're putting their trust. They work hard and earn money, trying to buy some measure of happiness. They seek security in insurance policies and alarm systems. They seem to worship cars, technology, and weekends. I'm not saying I'm any better than they are. You know how often I get swayed that way, but, Lord, I declare right now that you are my God. I want no other gods before you. You are the one.

July 18

*Lord, all my desire is before thee;
and my groaning is not hid from thee.*

—*Psalm 38:9*

Oh Lord, I could count my blessings and fill up a notepad or two, but you know the problems I have, too. Sometimes I sigh with deep dissatisfaction. Why couldn't things have turned out differently? My heart has plenty of regrets and remorse, and I do my share of coveting and gazing at the green grass on the other side of the fence. Ah, Lord, I take comfort in the fact that you know all that's in my heart—good and bad. Whisper your peace to me. Fill all my longings with your delightful presence.

July 19

*He that followeth after righteousness
and mercy findeth life,
righteousness, and honour.*

—Proverbs 21:21

213

July 20

Everything in my life lately seems to be going wrong. People are uncaring. Things I've worked hard for don't seem to be coming to fruition. Everyone needs my time and attention and I feel so tired and overwhelmed and stressed. I ask today in prayer for peace, for serenity. I don't ask for a removal of my problems, but for the power and fortitude to deal with them as they arise from a place of calm and stillness within. I know that you can provide me that kind of amazing, unerring peace, God. Be the rock upon which I can take comfort and rest when the world spins out of control all around me. Be my peace everlasting, dear God.

July 21

My heart is fixed, O God,
my heart is fixed:
I will sing and give praise.
Awake up, my glory;
awake, psaltery and harp:
I *myself* will awake early.

—Psalm 57:7–8

July 22

What has happened to me, Lord Jesus? I can't comprehend the calamity that has overwhelmed me. I still can't believe it happened to me. So many times on TV I've seen catastrophes happen to other people, and I felt deeply sorry for them, but I never thought it could happen to me. I can't stop repeating with disbelief, "It has happened to me! It has happened to me!" Lord, I know my zeal to serve you has not been as it should be, but I promise to be faithful to the leading of your Spirit. Just help me now, Lord! Please give me hope and strength to go on.

July 23

Behold, bless *ye* the Lord,
all ye servants of the Lord,
which by night stand
in the house of the Lord.
Lift up your hands *in* the sanctuary,
and bless the Lord.
—Psalm 134:1-2

July 24

I want to confess my attitudes of self-sufficiency to you, Father. As I seek you for help during this time of need, I realize how much I have neglected my relationship with you—how much I pushed you to the side, thinking there were more important things to pursue. I don't think you are trying to punish me for that; I just believe that in your mercy you intervened to stop me from getting too far away and getting lost in the shuffle of life. And you know, as bad as this financial situation has been, I am feeling more "on track" now that I've slowed down and have begun spending meaningful time with you, praying and reading your Word. It's good to be back.

July 25

And Jesus said, Somebody hath touched me:
for I perceive that virtue is gone out of me.
And when the woman saw
that she was not id, she came trembling,
and falling down before him, she declared
unto him before all the people
for what cause she had touched him,
and how she was healed immediately.
And he said unto her, Daughter,
be of good comfort:
thy faith hath made thee whole; go in peace.

—Luke 8:46-48

July 26

> For the Lord loveth judgment,
> and forsaketh not his saints;
> they are preserved for ever:
> but the seed of the wicked shall be cut off.
> —Psalm 37:28

If I believe God will keep me safe forever, what can my suffering in this life mean? It can only mean that I am not yet home. But God is faithfully leading me there to my eternal haven, keeping me safe from abandoning the path along the way through this sometimes painful but temporary journey.

July 27

Are you there, Lord? Are you? At times it seems that you're distant, and I'm not sure why. Have I strayed away from you? I don't think so. Have I offended you in some way? If so, I don't know how. I just don't feel the closeness we used to have. Is it just me, or is there a problem here? Maybe you don't want me to take you for granted. But because you have promised to be here for me always, I'm going to trust you to be with me, even when you're silent. If I have sinned, Lord, please let me know. If not, then just keep guiding me, even if that guidance is subtle. And please don't stop watching over me.

July 28

May your thoughts focus much more upon what you have than what you lack in this trying time. May your heart lay hold of present realities rather than future possibilities. For this moment—the now—is in front of us. Whether we are sick or healthy, this juncture in time is the place we share. Let us be blessed in this moment, safe in our knowledge of God's plan for us. Let us simply be in God's presence, just for this moment.

July 29

*For I am persuaded, that neither death,
nor life, nor angels, nor principalities,
nor powers, nor things present,
nor things to come, nor height,
nor depth, nor any other creature,
shall be able to separate us
from the love of God,
which is in Christ Jesus
our Lord.*
—Romans 8:38-39

July 30

But as for me, my prayer is unto thee,
O Lord, in an acceptable time:
O God, in the multitude
of thy mercy hear me,
in the truth of thy salvation.
Deliver me out of the mire,
and let me not sink:
let me be delivered from them that hate me,
and out of the deep waters.

—Psalm 69:13–14

July 31

*And he said unto her, Daughter,
thy faith hath made thee whole; go in peace,
and be whole of thy plague.*

—Mark 5:34

Heavenly Father, when I was young, I thought all things hurt or broken could be fixed: knees, feelings, bicycles, tea sets. Now I've learned that not everything can be repaired, relived, or cured. As a mother comforts her child, heal my hurting and grant me the peace I used to know. This I pray. Amen.

August

August 1

God, thank you for sometimes reminding me that in the center of chaos lies the seed of new opportunity and that things are not always as awful as they seem at first. I often forget that what starts out bad can end up great and that it is all a matter of my own perspective. Amen.

August 2

Crisis bargains with God are played for laughs or tears in movies, but in real life, these prayers can help us out of some serious jams. It's important to be thankful for the help we receive, whether it's a last-minute medical miracle or simply the calm we need to face the day.

August 3

We pray in desperate or troubling times, and these prayers can include promises to give up a bad habit or behavior. Why wait for a trial in order to make a pledge to God?

August 4

He will swallow up death in victory;
and the Lord God will wipe away tears
from off all faces;
and the rebuke of his people shall
he take away from off all the earth:
for the Lord hath spoken *it.*

—Isaiah 25:8

August 5

Thank you, Lord Jesus. Thank you for walking beside me on days when I'm too hurried and frazzled to think clearly. Thank you for softly saying to me, "Slow down. It's just not worth it." Thank you for reminding me that even you drew away from the demands of the world to rest and spend time with your heavenly Father. If you needed that kind of restoration, certainly I do, too. You and you alone can calm my spirit and restore my soul, and I want to listen and respond when you lead me away from the fray.

August 6

But the path of the just *is*
as the shining light,
that shineth more and more
unto the perfect day.
— *Proverbs 4:18*

Pray without ceasing,
let your love illumine the skies
That the darkness of man may drop away
And only the light of God show through.
Pray unto the Holy,
with all your heart and soul
Pray for the shining light of guidance
That your path may be glorious with love.
— St. Augustine

August 7

Dear God, as I rise each day, give me the strength, courage, and patience to do the best I can for my family. All through the day, guide me with your grace and divine direction into right action and right decision. And when the day is done and it is time for me to rest my weary mind and body, take the burden of my troubles from me so that I can sleep. Watch over me and mine throughout the night, and when it is time to arise to a new day, be there for me all over again. Amen.

August 8

Thou hast forgiven the iniquity of thy people,
thou hast covered all their sin.

—*Psalm 85:2*

August 9

God, grant me the courage to let go of shame, guilt, and anger. Free me of all negative energies, for only then will I become a conduit for joy and a channel for goodness. Amen.

August 10

I will be glad and rejoice in thy mercy:
for thou hast considered my trouble;
thou hast known my soul in adversities.

—Psalm 31:7

August 11

God with me lying down,
God with me rising up,
God with me in each ray of light
Nor I a ray of joy without Him,
Nor one ray without Him.

Christ with me sleeping,
Christ with me waking,
Christ with me watching,
Every day and night,
Each day and night.
God with me protecting,
The Lord with me directing,
The Spirit with me strengthening,
For ever and for evermore,
Ever and evermore,
Amen.

—Celtic Prayer

August 12

> *For whosoever shall call upon the name of the Lord shall be saved.*
>
> —Romans 10:13

The light that shines upon me,
The arms that reach to hold me,
The warmth that gives me comfort,
The angel's wings enfold me.
The word that gives me power,
The song that makes me whole,
The wisdom that empowers me,
The touch that heals my soul.

August 13

You said, Lord Jesus, in your Sermon on the Mount that the meek—the humble and lowly—will inherit the earth. This promise you've made assures me that you see how the world's system works, that you are not indifferent to the way power often becomes corrupt and abusive, and that you have a plan to set things right. Thank you that you wield your ultimate power in a way that defends the weak and needy and protects the poor and helpless. Help me reflect your heart today by standing with those whose hearts need strengthening and by standing up for those who are longing for justice.

August 14

Come to Christ to heal you.
He can in one moment make you whole.
Not in the sense of working
a sudden change in your feelings,
or in what you are in yourself,
but in the heavenly reality of coming in,
in response to your surrender and faith,
and taking charge of
your inner life,
and filling it with
Himself and Spirit.

—Rev. Andrew Murray

August 15

Sometimes the circumstances of our lives are so difficult, Lord! Often misfortunes seem to come all at once. Other times ongoing, wear-me-down situations or relationships seem to follow us day in and day out. Then there are the crushing tragedies that strike us in our tracks and devastate us. A life of faith is not defined by these things—but it is not exempt, either. Suffering is as real for the faithful as for anyone else. However, we have an "eternal comfort and good hope" that lifts us up. In that comfort and hope, God carries us, heals us with the balm of his tender mercies, and strengthens us to carry on in what is good.

August 16

For the Lord God will help me;
therefore shall I not be confounded:
therefore have I set my face like a flint,
and I know that I shall not be ashamed.

—Isaiah 50:7

August 17

The pain, heavenly Father, is more than I can bear. I cry out in agony, but the pain does not lessen. Tears do not help, either. Oh Father, please give me relief! Hear my prayers! Listen to my pleas! I desperately need your help. I can't take it any longer. The pain is too great for me. And yet, even in my misery, heavenly Father, I will praise you. You are a great God, and I place all my trust in you. This pain will not deter me from praising you. It will not lessen my faith in you. I will not falter, for you are my fortress. You are my sanctuary. I feel your hand of mercy on me now, and my gratitude is beyond words.

August 18

Yea, mine own familiar friend,
in whom I trusted,
which did eat of my bread,
hath lifted up his heel against me.
—Psalm 41:9

August 19

I feel the danger of too much solitude, Father. The more I am alone, the more used to being alone I become. Usually I enjoy going to worship services, but I'm beginning to be tempted to just stay home and not go through the effort of getting myself up and ready to participate. I begin to think I can have as meaningful a service in my own home, listening to the worship music that resonates best with my spirit, reading your Word on my own, maybe listening to a Bible teacher on TV. But I know your Word clearly says that I should not "forsake the assembling" together with other believers. There is something to it, and as long as I am able to, I will follow your direction on this.

August 20

Lord, so often we find ourselves asking you to save us from bad situations only to discover you quietly revealing to us that we are our own worst enemies! Teach us to break destructive habits and to stop polluting our minds with negative thoughts, Lord. Save us from our enemies, even when it means you have to step in and save us from ourselves!

August 21

And the prayer of faith shall save the
sick, and the Lord shall raise him up;
and if he have committed sins,
they shall be forgiven him.

— James 5:15

August 22

Lord, how I hate being sick! It's hard to function when I'm this way. Not only do I feel lousy, but I also don't want to spread my illness to others. And so, I feel both unwell and isolated, I suppose being sick and alone is a perfect time for me to commune with you—to share what I'm thinking and feeling and listen to what you want me to and do with my life. Thank you, Lord, for grabbing my attention is this way. Otherwise, I might be too busy to hear what you have to say to me. Please keep me grounded in you. I pray in Jesus' precious name. Amen.

August 23

Sometimes it seems that I'm fighting a losing battle. Life gets difficult, Lord, and it feels as if everyone and everything is against me. I seem to say the wrong thing. People misunderstand me. My daily work is harder than it should be. Even stoplights turned as I approach. What's going on? Is the entire universe my enemy? Well, no, you are still on my side, and you are much bigger and more powerful than the whole rest of the universe—besides, you made it! When the rest of my life becomes a struggle, I can still rely on your support. Thank you, Lord.

August 24

But I will sing of thy power;
yea, I will sing aloud
of thy mercy in the morning:
for thou hast been my defence
and refuge in the day of my trouble.

—Psalm 59:16

August 25

You were given the dreams you dream by a God who
knew you had the strength and fortitude to make
them come true. Go forth in his love and belief in
you. You can do this!

August 26

At the time I need strength,
God puts it in my heart or provides it
through someone who is close to me...
I don't earn it. I don't deserve it.
I don't bring it about. It's a gift.

—Dave Dravecky

August 27

Dear Lord, we live in a broken world. We need your touch. Heal us of our prejudices, our sicknesses, our compulsions, our hatreds, and our shortsightedness. Help us to see people as you see them. For that matter, help us see ourselves as you see us. Teach us to treat life as the gift you meant it to be. Keep us safe. Make us whole. Give us love to spare and forgiveness that can only come from you. Amen.

August 28

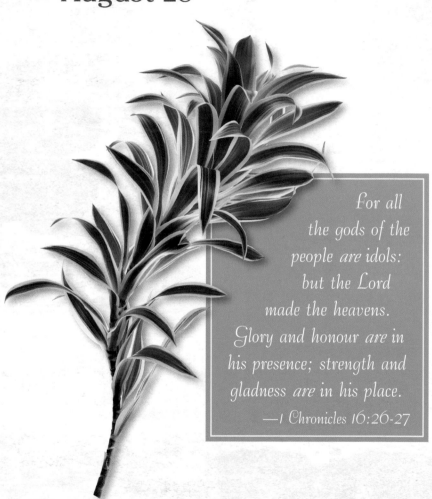

For all
the gods of the
people *are* idols:
but the Lord
made the heavens.
Glory and honour *are* in
his presence; strength and
gladness *are* in his place.
—1 Chronicles 16:26-27

August 29

Is there something new for me to learn in this imposed solitude, dear Lord? I know your Word says that there is a time and purpose for everything under heaven—even "a time to embrace and a time to refrain from embracing," according to the writer of Ecclesiastes. Well, Lord, I'm trying to trust that you have a purpose in this, but that purpose isn't clear to me, at least not yet. You know how much I am missing the "embrace" of human fellowship right now. Please let me sense the embrace of your fellowship more and more, not as a consolation prize but as the essence and source from which the best kind of fellowship can be had in this life. Help me be a good student, willing to learn as you work out your good purposes in my life.

August 30

The fear of the Lord *is* clean,
enduring for ever:
the judgments of the Lord *are* true
and righteous altogether.
More to be desired are *they* than gold,
yea, than much fine gold:
sweeter also than honey and
the honeycomb.

—Psalm 19:9–10

August 31

Teach me, teach me, dearest Jesus
In thine own sweet loving, way,
All the lessons of perfection
I must practice day by day.
Teach me meekness, dearest Jesus,
Of Thine own the counterpart;
Not in words and actions only,
But the meekness of the heart.
Teach, Humility, sweet Jesus
To this poor, proud heart of mine,
Which yet wishes, O my Jesus,
To be modeled after Thine.

—Reverend F. X. Lasance

September

September 1

The king shall joy in thy strength,
O Lord; and in thy salvation
how greatly shall he rejoice!
—Psalm 21:1

Out of sorrow the sweetest souls
have emerged. The most sympa-
thetic hearts are marked with scars
from wounds which have healed.
—Leroy Brownlow

September 2

And the Lord said unto him,
Now do ye Pharisees make clean
the outside of the cup and the platter;
but your inward part is full of ravening
and wickedness. Ye fools, did not he that
made that which is without make that
which is within also? But rather give alms
of such things as ye have; and, behold,
all things are clean unto you.

—Luke 11:39-41

September 3

We can give touch and comfort
and strength in physical healing,
but for spiritual healing we need
to turn to God. So, knowing our strengths
and our weaknesses, we turn to the Lord
because all of us carry our past hurts,
and He has the remedy for everything.
It's simple: If we just turn to Him,
He will bring us this inner healing,
this spiritual healing so we can make our lives
more holy and more pleasing to God.

—Sister Dolores,
quoted by Mother Teresa of Calcutta

September 4

Dear God,

I come to you today humbled and grateful for the powerful healing you have given me. I was so ill and broken, and weak in body and spirit, and I was losing my faith that I would ever feel good again. Yet you took care of me. Your love provided me with all the medicine I could ever need, and the hope of your eternal presence motivated me to stay in faith, even when things seemed so bleak. I thank you from the bottom of my heart for this new sense of well-being and health, and for knowing that if I stay positive and hopeful, your loving will for me will prevail over any disease or challenge. Amen.

September 5

Time helps, Lord, but it never quite blunts the lone-
liness that loss brings. Thank you for the peace that
is slowly seeping into my pores, allowing me to live
with the unlivable; to bear the unbearable.

Guide and bless my faltering steps down a new road.
Prop me up when I think I can't go it alone; prod me
when I tarry too long in lonely self-pity.

Most of all, Kind Healer, thank you for the gifts of
memory and dreams. The one comforts, the other
beckons, both halves of a healing whole.

September 6

You have the power, Lord, to heal me.
I don't doubt that for a minute.
You crafted me; you can recreate me.
I trust in your creative ability.
I know you love me.
You sent your beloved Son for my redemption.
And you shower me with blessings daily.
I trust in your love, Lord,
Your desire to bring me health.
It's a little harder to trust in your wisdom.
I think I know what I want here.
I know what my healing will look like, sort of.
But how do you want to pull that off?
Seriously, what's your idea of my wholeness?
How would you like to accomplish my healing?
I'm guessing you'll want to touch my mind, my soul,
My attitude, my relationships,
and—oh, yes—my health.
So let's do it, Lord.
I trust in your wisdom to heal all of me.
Amen.

September 7

> And *Jesus* went with him; and much people
> followed him, and thronged him.
>
> And a certain woman, which had an issue
> of blood twelve years, and had suffered many
> things of many physicians, and had spent
> all that she had, and was nothing bettered,
> but rather grew worse, when she had heard
> of Jesus, came in the press behind,
> and touched his garment. For she said,
> If I may touch but his clothes,
> I shall be whole. And straightway
> the fountain of her blood was dried up;
> and she felt in her body that
> she was healed of that plague.
>
> —Mark 5:24-29

September 8

Dear God,

I pray today to have more faith in my own abilities.
I sometimes sell myself short and don't go out on a
limb, afraid to fail at something even if I really want
to try it. I let doubt scare me away and talk myself
out of things, sure I don't have what it takes to make
them happen. Then I regret never having gone after
my dreams or feeling accomplished. I know that
you have faith in me, but how do I find that faith for
myself? Help me to recognize my own worth and
strength, and to see that I am far more capable than
I imagine myself to be. Help me to reach above and
beyond where I am to get to where I want to be and
to feel happy and fulfilled again. Amen.

September 9

*Fear none of those things
which thou shalt suffer: behold,
the devil shall cast some of you into prison,
that ye may be tried;
and ye shall have tribulation ten days:
be thou faithful unto death,
and I will give thee a crown of life.*

—*Revelation 2:10*

September 10

Dear God,

Not a day goes by, dear God, when your faith in me doesn't show up as some small miracle in my life. I am in awe of your belief in me, even when I don't believe in myself. Your loving grace gives me the courage to do anything, and your trust in me strengthens my resolve. I am so grateful you see me through the eyes of a loving Father, and you never let me down or abandon me in my times of need. Thank you, God, for the faith that can move mountains, and for helping me to realize that with you beside me, all those mountains are nothing more than large hills that can be easily climbed. I cherish your faith in me, God. Amen.

September 11

> *The fear of man bringeth a snare:*
> *but whoso putteth his trust*
> *in the Lord shall be safe.*
>
> —*Proverbs* 29:25

Dear Lord,

Thank you for the courage you've given me to pursue my dreams. So many of my friends have settled for lives filled with regrets and unfulfilled dreams, and I've been so blessed by you with the inner fire and drive to take my divinely-given talents and do something with them. No matter how hard I worked, I knew that I could not achieve such goals without you and I've always strived to keep your presence close at hand in all my decisions and choices. Thank you, Lord, for helping me find that extra strength within to face my fears, my doubts and my insecurities and go for a life well-lived. Amen.

September 12

And it came to pass, as he went to Jerusalem, that he passed through the midst of Samaria and Galilee. And as he entered into a certain village, there met him ten men that were lepers, which stood afar off: and they lifted up their voices, and said, Jesus, Master, have mercy on us. And when he saw them, he said unto them, Go shew yourselves unto the priests. And it came to pass, that, as they went, they were cleansed.

—Luke 17:11-14

September 13

Dear Lord,

I ask in prayer today for courage and strength to face some big challenges before me. I admit I am anxious, and even afraid, but I know in my heart you will never give me anything I cannot handle, and that you will be by my side the whole way. Instill in me a strong heart and spirit as I deal with my problems and keep my mind centered and focused on the solutions you set before me. I ask nothing more than your presence alongside me as I overcome these obstacles and learn the lessons each one has for my life. I thank you, Lord, for always being there for me in my times of need and struggle. Amen.

September 14

My life is full of ah-hahs.
Born during the hottest part
of seventy summers ago nurtured
in a mother's love anchored
by a father's strength adventured
in childhood joys searched
for identity traveled abroad yearned
for Mr. Right married mothered
a darling baby grieved
her early death suffered the pain,
weathered the agony and now
having a love affair with life!

—Bee Jay

September 15

There is a balm in Gilead
To make the wounded whole;
There is a balm in Gilead
To heal the sin-sick soul.
Some times I feel discouraged,
And think my work's in vain,
But then the Holy Spirit
Revives my soul again.
If you can't preach like Peter,
If you can't pray like Paul,
Just tell the love of Jesus,
And say He died for all.
There is a balm in Gilead
To make the wounded whole;
There is a balm in Gilead
To heal the sin-sick soul.

—African American spiritual

September 16

God, we know that pain has produced some wisdom
in our lives, but it has also created cynicism and fear.
People turn on us, reject us, hurt us, and none of
us wants to play the fool more than once, so we're
tempted to close off our hearts to people and to you.
But relationships that bring meaning and joy require
vulnerability. Help us trust you to be our truest
friend and to lead us to the kind of community that
will bring healing rather than destruction.

September 17

I know not of what the future hath
Of marvel or surprise,
Assured alone that life and death
His mercy underlies.
And if my heart and flesh are weak
To bear an untried pain
The bruised reed he will not break,
But strengthen and sustain.
. . . I know not where his islands lift
Their fronded palms in air;
I only know I cannot drift
Beyond his love and care.

—John Greenleaf Whittier,
"The Eternal Goodness"

September 18

So please don't think I'm heroic.
I've had just as much trouble adjusting
to all of this as any of you would have.
In fact, at first I almost gave up and went
back home. It was a struggle to see
underneath the rags and smells,
the human beings—some with fine minds,
some with great spirits, lovable,
proud, sensitive—and begin to care
about them, really care.

It's like—well, like garden vegetables.
If you threw out your turnips
because they came out of the ground
with dirt clinging to them,
you'd never discover the goodness there.

—Catherine Marshall

September 19

And what if healing does not come to us?
Even then we do not need
to lose heart nor faith.
We will believe that God's grace is sufficient,
that his power is made perfect in weakness.
We shall look up,
lift up our heads,
and look for the coming King.
With his coming will come also complete
wholeness and vibrant health.

— Mildred Tengbom

September 20

*Therefore whosoever
heareth these sayings
of mine, and doeth them,
I will liken him unto a wise man,
which built his house upon a rock:
and the rain descended, and the floods came,
and the winds blew,
and beat upon that house; and it fell not:
for it was founded upon a rock.*

—Matthew 7:24-25

God is bigger than any problem you have. Whoever is opposing you is a weakling compared to God. Why not tap into God's supply of strength? Why focus on your problem when God is so much more interesting?

September 21

A woman's life is filled with challenges. But there is nothing stronger than a woman with the will of God within to help her hold steady to what is good, right, and just. A woman persists with the courage of a warrior and the heart of a nurturer. A woman overcomes with God at her side.

September 22

We can take a lesson from the precious water lily. For no matter what outside force or pressure is put upon the lily, it always rises back to the water's surface again to feel the nurturing sunlight upon its leaves and petals. We must be like the lily, steadfast and true in the face of every difficulty, that we too may rise above our problems and feel God's light upon our faces again.

September 23

Lord Jesus, you are medicine
to me when I am sick,
strength to me when I need help,
life itself when I fear death,
the way when I long for heaven,
the light when all is dark,
and food when I need nourishment.
Glory be to you forever. Amen.

—Saint Ambrose

September 24

And lest I should be exalted above measure
through the abundance of the revelations,
there was given to me a thorn in the flesh,
the messenger of Satan to buffet me,
lest I should be exalted above measure.
For this thing I besought the Lord thrice,
that it might depart from me.
And he said unto me, My grace is sufficient
for thee: for my strength is made perfect in
weakness. Most gladly therefore will I
rather glory in my infirmities,
that the power of Christ may rest upon me.
Therefore I take pleasure in infirmities,
in reproaches, in necessities, in persecutions,
in distresses for Christ's sake:
for when I am weak, then am I strong.

—2 Corinthians 12:7-10

September 25

My mom died of cancer when I was still in college. She was diagnosed with a brain tumor in the spring, and was gone before Christmas. My dad was devastated and in his grief, withdrew from the world; he could not be there for us kids to lean on emotionally. It was a very difficult time in my life; what got me through was the support I received at the church in my college town. In what was probably the loneliest time in my life, I was nevertheless surrounded by love. Various members of the congregation invited me over for home-cooked meals or pizza-and-movie nights. These folks encouraged me that God was still there, and through their loving actions, I experienced God's grace. God is with us even when we feel alone.

September 26

Grace of my heart, I turn to you when I am feeling lost and alone. You restore me with strength and hope and the courage to face a new day. You bless me with joy and comfort me through trials and tribulations. You direct my thoughts, guide my actions, and temper my words. You give me the patience and kindness I need to be good. Grace of my heart, I turn to you. Amen.

September 27

But unto you that fear my name
shall the Sun of righteousness arise
with healing in his wings;
and ye shall go forth,
and grow up as calves of the stall.

— *Malachi 4:2*

Whatever the relationship, forgiveness
is a truly healing gift for the people
involved. In a marriage, the power of
true forgiveness cannot be overstated.

September 28

Dear God,

There are times when I act small in the world because I'm afraid to get out of my comfort zone. I'm scared of looking foolish, or failing terribly and letting people down. Yet, you've given me talents and abilities and I long to use them for good in the world. Help me, God, to find that courageous lion within me, and to go forward with trust and inner strength, knowing that whatever comes up, you'll help me through it. I pray for your will to be done in my life, and for the fearlessness that comes from having you as my rock and my foundation. Let me shine my light, God, and help me not play it safe and miss out on the incredible experiences you have in store for me. Amen.

September 29

If you want to comfort others,
let God first comfort you,
and then share that comfort.
But keep in mind that comfort
is more than "sympathy."
Our English word comfort comes
from two Latin words that
together mean "with strength."
The Greek word Paul used means
"to come alongside to help."
Our word encouragement means
"to put heart into."
In other words, we comfort people,
not by unanswerable arguments,
but by unfailing love and acceptance.

—Warren Wiersbe,
Why Us? When Bad Things Happen to God's People

September 30

I never meant to be a failure, O God of covenants and promises. I never meant to break vows solemnly made. But I am and I did. Comfort me as I mourn the truth that I could not be okay and remain in that marriage. Comfort me as I leave behind the familiar—friends, surroundings, assumptions, home, and connections. I also lose all of them in this "settlement." Lead me toward other friends and new landmarks, but let this new life not be created quickly and casually, Lord, as if divorce is no more serious than clipping one's fingernails. Enable me to learn something from this grieving passage so that my mistakes don't get repeated and I roll out of one non-okay marriage into another without missing a beat. Be with me now, Lord, as I leave not only a familiar place, but a familiar me. Grant me wisdom to go forward now, toward a new home and life, solitary but free. Be with me; the way home has never seemed longer.

October

October 1

Love the Lord your God,
and love one another.
Love one another as he loves.
Love with strength and purpose
and passion and no matter
what comes against you.
Don't weaken.
Stand against the darkness and love.
That's the way back
into Eden.
That's the way back to life.

—Francine Rivers

October 2

*My brethren, count it all joy when ye
fall into divers temptations; knowing this,
that the trying of your faith worketh patience.
But let patience have her perfect work,
that ye may be perfect and entire,
wanting nothing.*

—James 1:2-4

Where there is lack, Faith shouts "Abundance!"
Where there is despair, Faith sings out, "Joy!" Where
there is fear, Faith whispers "Courage." Where there
is animosity, Faith affirms only LOVE.

October 3

He giveth power to the faint;
and to *them that have* no might
he increaseth strength.

—Isaiah 40:29

Thank you for some release, some sleep.
I will be an instrument of your love.
Now I am in need of tremendous strengthening.
I implore. Give me your strength for my body.
Fill me anew with your joy and love.
I need help in so many things.
Yard is overrun. House needs painting . . .
I am so tired. Completely depleted.

—Karen Burton Mains

October 4

The night is given us to take breath,
to pray, to drink deep at the fountain
of power. The day, to use the strength
which has been given us, to go forth
to work with it till the evening.

—Florence Nightingale

The resilient heart withstands the winds of
change, just as the flexible branch of a tree
bends but does not break.

October 5

When life's winds toss me
upon the waves of uncertainty and doubt,
And when the tempest beats me
and rocks of guilt and self-pity,
When my pitiful heart yearns
for love I cannot find,
When the darkness seems darker
and the night longer,
Some unseen hand reaches down,
and with a strength and tenderness
I cannot comprehend,
Pulls me back into the light.

October 6

> *And I thank Christ Jesus our Lord,*
> *who hath enabled me,*
> *for that he counted me faithful,*
> *putting me into the ministry.*
>
> —*1 Timothy 1:12*

You never have to walk alone through life, because God walks with you. Whether your path is smooth and free of obstacles, or rough and filled with detours, God is there to help guide you and give you the strength to carry on and keep moving forward. There is no reason to feel lonely, and there is nothing to fear. God is there, now and always.

October 7

Though you may stumble and fall along the way,
God will be at your side to offer you a hand up.
Though you may weep with sadness and suffer in
pain, God is there to comfort you and bring healing.
No matter what you are going through, God is there
to help, to hold, to heal, and to love you.

October 8

When God wants to move a mountain,
he does not take a bar of iron,
but he takes a little worm.
The fact is, we have too much strength.
We are not weak enough.
It is not our strength that we want.
One ounce of God's strength is worth
more than all the world.

—Dwight L. Moody

When we are lonely and sad, we forget that we have a lion within each of us to call upon. That lion is bold, courageous, strong, and unafraid. That lion gives us the extra confidence we need to keep moving, even when we want to stay still. Listen to the lion inside and find courage. Then go forth and roar! God did not make us to play small and weak.

October 9

Today may you come to acceptance. What is, is. May you find blessed relief in seeing—without judging, being—without having to become, knowing—without needing to change a thing. Then, should you be healed, it will be a gracious, unexpected surprise. May you soon arrive at perfect acceptance.

October 10

O God, healing is going so-o-o-o slowly, and I am impatient and grumpy. Mind, body, or soul, this could take a long time. Remind me that recovery is a journey, not a hasty jet-lagged arrival. Bless me with faith to sustain me, step by small step. You do miraculous things with faith as tiny as mustard seeds that, in time, blossom into awesome growth. I hold that picture as I make progress along the road to healing.

October 11

For my part, I will sing of your strength;
I will celebrate your love in the morning;
For you have become my stronghold,
A refuge in the day of my trouble.
To you, O my Strength will I sing;
For you, O God are my stronghold
and my merciful God.

—The Book of Common Prayer

May you be healed, in mind, body, and soul. May you come to know that all healing proceeds from God, and he cares about every part of you. Perhaps the healing will come sooner for your attitude than for your body. Perhaps your mind will experience peace quicker than bones and muscles. But sooner or later, all will be well.

October 12

We're stained, like a paint rag, by troubles we caused ourselves, Lord. Red, the color of lost temper and rudeness. Green, envy of others who have it easier and more of it. Blue, the shade of despair over something we could change. Yellow, of cowardly running. Rearrange our unsightly smudges into glorious rainbows through your gift of forgiveness.

October 13

Dear God,

Give me the wisdom to know what is important in life, and the courage to pursue those things. My life is such a blur lately, with an overload of obligations, information and distractions coming at me to the point where I end up feeling so tired and worn down. I'm not getting things done, and failing to take care of my own health. Help me slow down and focus, and not be afraid to say no. Give me strength to tackle the important duties, which then leave room for more fun in my life. Show me, God, balance and harmony between what I need to do for others, and what I need to replenish myself. Amen.

October 14

The Lord is my strength and song,
and he is become my salvation:
he is my God,
and I will prepare him an habitation;
my father's God, and I will exalt him.

—Exodus 15:2

If we could stop pretending to be strong
and start being honest with ourselves and
God, crying out, "God, please help! I
am poor and needy," He would hurry to
help us and be the strength of our lives.

October 15

*A wholesome tongue is a tree of life:
but perverseness therein is a breach
in the spirit.*

—*Proverbs 15:4*

When I operate from my own will, I grow
tired and weary. When I accept God's
will, I feel as though the floodgates have
opened and I am floating downstream,
relaxed and in the flow of blessings!

October 16

Faith makes all evil good to us,
and all good better; unbelief makes
all good evil, and all evil worse.
Faith laughs at the shaking of the spear;
unbelief trembles at the shaking of a leaf,
unbelief starves the soul; faith finds food
in famine, and a table in the wilderness.
In the greatest danger, faith said,
"I have a great God." When outward
strength is broken, faith rests on the promises.
In the midst of sorrow, faith draws the string
out of every trouble, and takes out
the bitterness from every affliction.

—Robert Cecil

October 17

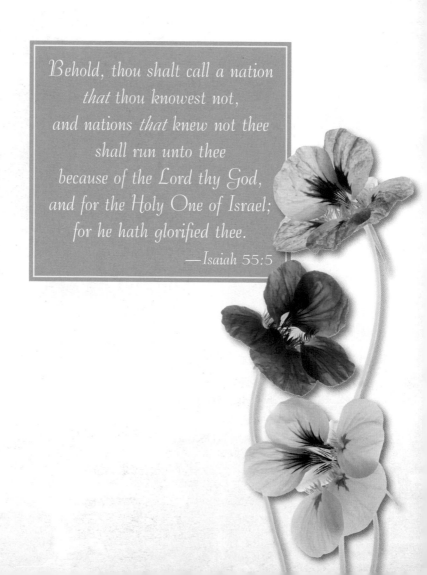

Behold, thou shalt call a nation
that thou knowest not,
and nations *that* knew not thee
shall run unto thee
because of the Lord thy God,
and for the Holy One of Israel;
for he hath glorified thee.

—Isaiah 55:5

October 18

*Lord, we pray for the power
to be gentle;
the strength to be forgiving;
the patience to be understanding;
and the endurance to accept
the consequences of holding
to what we believe to be right.*

*—Week of Prayer for World Peace,
Oxford Book of Prayer*

When my own strength fails me, I turn to God.
When my heart quivers in fear, I turn to God.
When I am scared and don't know what to do
next, I turn to God. There are times when my
own strength is enough, but when it isn't, I
know that God is always present to pick me up
with I fall and carry me. With God at my side,
my fear vanishes and my courage returns.

October 19

In the midst of the street of it,
and on either side of the river,
was there the tree of life,
which bare twelve *manner of fruits*,
and yielded her fruit every month:
and the leaves of the tree *were*
for the healing of the nations.
—*Revelation 22:2*

Lord, I want to leave the fighting behind us. It's time to begin the healing process. Show me how to reconcile and how to be humble without being a doormat. I want the respect we have had for one another to remain intact. Amen.

October 20

Then touched he their eyes, saying,
According to your faith be it unto you.
And their eyes were opened;
and Jesus straitly charged them,
saying, See *that* no man know *it.*

—*Matthew 9:29-30*

Choose your words carefully, for they can become
stepping stones to healing.

October 21

Giver of life and all good gifts:
Grant us also wisdom
to use only what we need;
Courage to trust your bounty;
Imagination to preserve our resources;
Determination to deny frivolous excess;
And inspiration to sustain
through temptation.

—Patricia Winters

October 22

October 23

Dear Lord,

Guide my steps today so that I might help others and be a light in the world, especially for those who are weak and troubled. I pray for the courage to stand against injustices and to reach out to my fellow humans without fear or concern of the repercussions. I am ready to be a force for good, Lord. I am willing to step into a purpose that is founded in love and in spreading that love to all I meet. All I ask is that you direct my actions and keep me strong and pure in spirit. Amen.

October 24

*And the people, when they knew it,
followed him: and he received them,
and spake unto them of the kingdom of God,
and healed them that had need of healing.*

—Luke 9:11

O God of rest and rejuvenation, guide me to find
ways to let your nurturing reach me. I need to be
healthy and well-rested in order to provide, lead, and
inspire. Burning the candle at both ends all the time is
hardly an example I'm proud of.

October 25

Suffering refines our faith.
The trivial is excised,
the essential emphasized.
Do we believe God in the face of it all?
If so, we will grow and be strengthened.
Suffering prepares us to comfort others.
Words from smiling, indifferent faces
to wounded hearts mean little;
but words from a fellow
sufferer support and uplift.
Suffering removes artificial
props of security and resets the
stage of our personal world
with new dependence
on Christ.

—Charles Stanley

October 26

I never meant to be a failure, Lord, never meant to break commitments. But I am and I did. Comfort me, for I mourn the loss of innocence that crumbled beneath the knowledge that I couldn't stay in the marriage and be okay. Forgive my failures; heal my regrets and fortify my courage. Help me grieve and go on free from toxic, wasteful hate. And as I do, help me forgive those left behind.

October 27

For this cause we also, since the day
we heard it, do not cease to pray for you,
and to desire that ye might be filled
with the knowledge of his will in all wisdom
and spiritual understanding; that ye might
walk worthy of the Lord unto all pleasing,
being fruitful in every good work,
and increasing in the knowledge of God;
strengthened with all might,
according to his glorious power,
unto all patience and longsuffering
with joyfulness; giving thanks
unto the Father, which hath made us meet
to be partakers of the inheritance
of the saints in light.

—Colossians 1:9–12

October 28

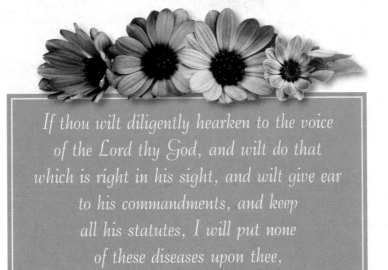

If thou wilt diligently hearken to the voice of the Lord thy God, and wilt do that which is right in his sight, and wilt give ear to his commandments, and keep all his statutes, I will put none of these diseases upon thee, which I have brought upon the Egyptians: for I am the Lord that healeth thee.

—*Exodus 15:26*

God, let me thank you for all of the times you've pushed me forward when I wanted to stop. For the days when I thought I could not continue, thank you for giving me the shove I needed to break on through. With you, I can go on and fight the good fight!

October 29

If you do a good job for others,
you heal yourself at the same,
because a dose of joy is a spiritual cure.

—Dietrich Bonhoeffer

When feelings are hurt, Wise Physician, we curl in
on ourselves like orange rinds, withholding even
the possibility of reconciliation. Help us open up to
new possibilities for righting wrong and sharing love
without reservation, as the orange blossom offers its
fragrance, the fruit of its zesty sweetness.

October 30

God gives us strength to go with our friends and share their burdens and responsibilities. When my friend and mentor, Diane, needed to travel to a cancer clinic in another city, I felt called to accompany her. I could not change her diagnosis, but I could be there, as a friend and companion, as she has been there for me these many years.

October 31

Peace I leave with you,
my peace I give unto you:
not as the world giveth,
give I unto you.
Let not your heart be troubled,
neither let it be afraid.

—John 14:27

Bless and use our reclamation efforts, for it is a task we can't accomplish alone. With your help, we can bind up and reclaim this poor old earth. We feel whispers of hope in the winds of changed hearts and minds, for we recall your promise to make all things new—even this earth we shall yet learn to tend. We are grateful for another chance.

November

November 1

Life is filled with experiences that require us to reach deep within and find our courage. When fear threatens to keep us from trying something new, we can tap into that inner courage, which is God's presence, and find our footing. We may still be afraid, but we go forward anyway, knowing we will be given all we need to take on the challenge and tackle any new situation.

November 2

Lord, remind us of a childhood memory of someone in uniform who made a difference in our lives.
A school nurse who comforted us, a firefighter who
spoke to us on a field trip to the local station, a police
officer standing on the neighborhood corner, a doctor
who treated us for a childhood illness. Thank you for
showing us that someone in uniform could be trusted
and could be a friend.

November 3

*And Judas and Silas,
being prophets also themselves,
exhorted the brethren with many words,
and confirmed them.*

—Acts 15:32

November 4

Chances are you limit yourself in life because of fear and doubt. But God says you can do all things through him. God strengthens you and empowers you to break through those limitations and experience a joyful life. Even if you are afraid, go ahead and do it anyway and you will find God there to give you wings to soar with.

November 5

Strengthen ye the weak hands,
and confirm the feeble knees.

—Isaiah 35:3

I will not turn back. I will not
give up. I will never surrender.
With God at my side, I will
simply step over obstacles, go
around challenges, and break
through blocks put in my path.
With God, I am unstoppable!

November 6

Though Marilyn loves to sing, she sometimes can't stay in tune. When she was a child, her choir instructor would often tell her to "just mouth the words." Marilyn became shy about her voice; it wasn't until years later, when her boyfriend Erik came upon her singing hymns in the kitchen, that she was encouraged to express herself again in song. "Singing makes me happy," Marilyn says. "Erik reminded me that God doesn't care if I'm note perfect!" Dear Lord, you embolden us to speak out in many ways, one of which is the gift of song. May I never fear that my song is not sweet enough!

November 7

Feel the fear and do it anyway, for you will find you
have more inner strength than you ever imagined. Call
upon God to be there, should you fall, and go ahead
and try. You may find out that you had the ability to
do it alone all along, but isn't it good to know that
when you can't, God is there to back you up?

November 8

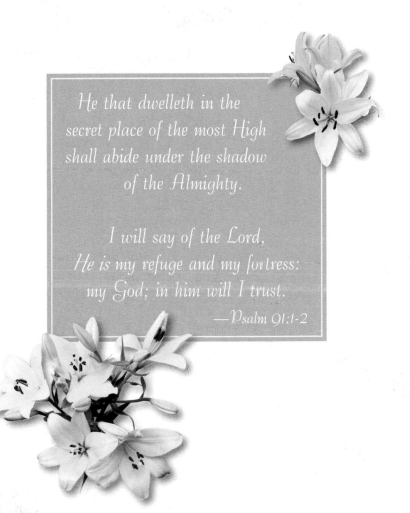

He that dwelleth in the
secret place of the most High
shall abide under the shadow
of the Almighty.

I will say of the Lord,
He is my refuge and my fortress:
my God; in him will I trust.

—Psalm 91:1-2

November 9

The Lord *is* good,
a strong hold in the
day of trouble;
and he knoweth them
that trust in him.

—Nahum 1:7

November 10

One of the greatest gifts in life is being able to be there for someone who is suffering. Sharing our strength, hope, and courage with those that are feeling weak is a blessing for all involved. The gift of service in the form of being someone else's pillar of strength, something they can lean on when their own legs fail them, is such a powerful experience of love in action.

November 11

> There hath no temptation taken you
> but such as is common to man:
> but God is faithful, who will not suffer you
> to be tempted above that ye are able;
> but will with the temptation
> also make a way to escape,
> that ye may be able to bear it.
>
> —1 Corinthians 10:13

Show me a sign, dear God, to help me figure out this problem I am struggling with. Give me something my spirit will recognize to help me overcome what stands in the way of my happiness. Help me, God, to see your solution as the calm within the storm.

November 12

*It is God that
girdeth me with strength,
and maketh my way perfect.*
—Psalm 18:32

November 13

> *The Lord thy God in the midst*
> *of thee is mighty;*
> *he will save, he will rejoice over thee with joy;*
> *he will rest in his love,*
> *he will joy over thee with singing.*
>
> —*Zephaniah 3:17*

In my hours of weakness, I reach out to others for the strength to carry on. In my times of need, I ask for help from others, and their love gives me the courage to keep going. God has given us the gift of other people not just to love us, but also to be there for us when we cannot make it on our own.

November 14

Lord, we've tossed our prayers aloft, and hopefully, expectantly, we wait for your answers. As we do, we will: listen, for you speak in the voice of nature; see you as a companion in the face and hand of a friend; feel you as a sweet-smelling rain, a river breeze; believe you can provide encouragement, direction, and guidance for those who have only to ask. We feel your presence.

November 15

Some days the race feels like a sprint, Lord, and on other days, a marathon. I want to press on, but I need you to infuse my spirit with your strength and steadfastness. I want to run and finish well. Thank you for beginning the work of faith in my life and for promising not to stop working until my faith is complete.

November 16

Dear God, I ask today for a bold new vision for my life. I ask for the strength and wisdom to be a better person to all those I come in contact with. I ask for the courage to step out of my comfort zone and expand my capacity for joy.

November 17

When the storms of life surround us, Lord, we cannot see the light of the sun behind the clouds, and so we forget it is there. The winds blow hard upon us, and the cold air chills us, but once the storm has passed, we stand in the sun again, and we find we have been cleansed.

November 18

Life has taught me to think,
but thinking has not taught me
how to live.

— Alexander Herzen

When I feel weak, tired, and alone,
give me strength, God, to stand up
and face the challenges before me with
hope, grace, and the power that comes
from your presence. Help me, God,
to find the courageous lion within.

November 19

*And ye shall serve the Lord your God,
and he shall bless thy bread, and thy water;
and I will take sickness away
from the midst of thee.*

—*Exodus 23:25*

Bless those who tend us when we are ailing in body, mind, and soul. They are a gift from you, Great Healer, sent to accompany us along the scary roads of illness. Bless their skills, potions, and bedside manners. Sustain them as they sustain us, for they are a channel of your love.

November 20

God.
God is.
God is holy.
God is personal and close.
God is there; God is here.
God is spirit.
God is.
God.

Gentle
healers
of mind,
body, and spirit are
surely a gift from you
sent to travel lonely
roads as our com-
panions. Sustain
them as they
sustain us; they
are a channel of
your love.

November 21

Healing has many faces:
The easing of tension,
The relaxing of frown lines,
The sigh of relief,
The softening in the eyes,
The quickening of the spirit,
The return of laughter.

Life goes back and
forth between push
and pull, force and
acceptance, fight
and surrender. It's
exhausting! But
staying in God's
will makes the doors
of life open easier
and more frequently
than when we rely
only on ourselves.

November 22

Blest feast of love divine!
'Tis grace that makes us free
to feed upon this bread and wine,
in memory Lord of thee.
That blood which flowed for sin,
in symbols here we see,
and feel the blessed pledge within
that we are loved by thee.

—Sir Edward Denny

November 23

When the anguish of loss
overwhelms us,
and we feel there's no
reason to live.
We must look deep
within to find meaning
and to know we've still
so much to give.

God, the knowledge
that your promises will
be fulfilled keeps me
going through the tough-
est of days and nights. I
know if I stay strong and
power through, I will be
richly rewarded in body,
mind, and spirit.

November 24

As you face death with all its impact
on your feelings and your way of life,
the greatest force for sustaining you
and bringing meaning to the apparently
meaningless is your ability to see life not
with physical preoccupations but in the light
of the New Testament revelation.

—Edgar N. Jackson

November 25

O spread the tidings 'round,
wherever man is found,
wherever human hearts
and human woes abound;
let every Christian tongue proclaim
the joyful sound:
The Comforter has come!
The Comforter has come,
the Comforter has come!
The Holy Ghost from heaven,
the Father's promise given;
O spread the tidings 'round,
wherever man is found—
the Comforter has come!
The long, long night is past,
the morning breaks at last,
and hushed the dreadful wail
and fury of the blast,
as over the golden hills the day advances fast!
The Comforter has come!

—Frank Bottome

November 26

*And I will bring the blind by a way
that they knew not;
I will lead them in paths
that they have not known:
I will make darkness light before them,
and crooked things straight.
These things will I do unto them,
and not forsake them*

—Isaiah 42:16

Lord God, I am about to throw in the towel! I can't go on without your strength to get me over the edge and into the light again. Help me remember why I chose these goals and dreams to begin with, God. Keep me strong to the finish!

November 27

Every good thing that comes into our lives carries within it the power to make us fear its loss. Yet, at those distressing times when we lose our grip on the things we think will save us, there is something beyond the fear. It is the recognition that loss can carry hope along with it: the hope that what is taken away will be replaced by something even better.

— Joseph Biuso and Brian Newman

In my hour of need, I turn my eyes inward to a place where God's strength flows like a river of healing waters. I immerse myself in the current, and I am renewed.

November 28

*Wherefore comfort yourselves together,
and edify one another, even as also ye do.*

—1 Thessalonians 5:11

God made me a woman and God made me strong.
I can be a mother, a lover, a friend, a sister, a daughter, and a caring and compassionate leader. I can do anything with God's presence as my power. I can be anything with God at my side!

November 29

Dark days do not last forever. The clouds are always moving, through very slowly. The person in the midst of depression is certain, of course, that the clouds are not moving . . . One of the most helpful things we can do for a friend at such a time is to stand by that friend in quiet confidence, and assure him or her that this, too, shall pass.

—Granger E. Westberg

Dearest God, my body is slowing, and I am in need of healing. I am scared of illness and of what lies ahead. I ask now for your healing light to shine upon me and favor me with your grace. I ask now for your love. I give myself to you, God, and I pray that you will help me and heal me.

November 30

Somebody said that it couldn't be done,
But he with a chuckle replied
That "maybe it couldn't" but he would be one
Who wouldn't say so till he'd tried.
So he buckled right in with the trace of a grin
On his face. If he worried he hid it.
He started to sing as he tackled the thing
That couldn't be done, and he did it.
There are thousands to tell you
it cannot be done,
There are thousands who prophesy failure;
There are thousands to point out to
you one by one,
The dangers that wait to assail you.
But just buckle in with a bit of a grin,
Just take off your coat and go to it;
Just start in to sing as you tackle the thing
That "cannot be done," and you'll do it.

—Edgar Guest

December

December 1

My faith looks up to thee
Thou Lamb of Calvary,
Savior Divine
Now hear me while I pray;
Take all my guilt away
O let me from this day
be wholly Thine.
—Ray Palmer

When the night is dark and cold, and the days promise little rest, be strong, because God has made you a promise of a mighty kingdom on the other side. Work hard, keep moving, and never let others derail you from your mission.

December 2

Lord, no matter what our personal battles are this holiday season, we rest assured that you are with us every moment. Family relationships can be strained this time of year. Feelings can be easily trampled. But what better time to focus on all the blessings we have (even if some of them come in the form of difficult relatives!). Deliver us from any ill will, Lord, and keep us focused on all the reasons we have to be thankful.

December 3

Now when Job's three friends heard
of all this evil that was come upon him,
they came every one from his own place;
Eliphaz the Temanite,
and Bildad the Shuhite,
and Zophar the Naamathite:
for they had made an appointment together
to come to mourn with him
and to comfort him.

—Job 2:11

December 4

Sometimes it's good for me to just step back and look at the whole picture of who you are, Lord—to remember your greatness and meditate on all the implications of it. When I look at how big you are, my problems that seemed so gigantic a few moments ago suddenly seem almost silly. My big plans seem less important, and my high notions of myself get cut down to size. I come away not feeling diminished, though—rather lifted up in spirit and full of faith and gratitude. Surely we were made to praise you, Lord!

December 5

Where no counsel *is*, the people fall: but in the multitude of counsellors there is safety.

—*Proverbs 11:14*

Dear Lord, grant me the humility to seek—and listen to!—the counsel of others. Grant me the wisdom to surround myself with wise friends.

December 6

Lord, how important it is for us to be thankful at all times. It's so easy to fall into the trap of having specific expectations and then despairing when events take an unexpected turn. You are working in our lives every moment, Lord. We will do our part by working hard and taking full advantage of all opportunities that come our way, but we also know that some matters are reserved for you. We are thankful that nothing is beyond your control, Lord, and we are grateful that you are our wise leader.

December 7

*But seek ye first the kingdom of God,
and his righteousness;
and all these things shall be added unto you.*
—*Matthew 6:33*

How much happier and at peace would we be if we allowed God to order our days? If we just focus on the promises of his love for us, all else will fall into place accordingly, without our exhausting effort.

December 8

The first step toward accomplishing any goal is to make a plan. Ask God to help you lay the blueprint for your dream, for he knows best the right tools to use, and the strongest materials to build with.

December 9

When I follow God's will and do as he instructs me, my direction becomes clear as I step out onto the path. I look around and see his presence everywhere, guiding me forward to where my spirit longs to be. I see his signs showing me the way.

December 10

*Open thy mouth, judge righteously,
and plead the cause of the poor and needy.*

—Proverbs 31:9

When you need a helping hand, look around for the angels God has placed in your path. Human angels come in the form of friends, mentors, and even strangers with words meant just for you to hear. Reach out, look, and receive God's blessings through his earthly angels.

December 11

Serena and her husband Jim moved to their new home during winter, and she'd looked forward to the neighborhood's annual summer block party. She figured she'd meet new people; what she didn't anticipate was that her faith might be challenged. "So you're one of those religious types?" a woman laughed, upon learning that Serena and Jim attended a church nearby. Though uncomfortable, Serena dug deep: "Yes," she responded with polite firmness. "We've found happiness in our new church home." Dear Lord, sometimes I am asked to justify my faith; sometimes I am even mocked for it. Please strengthen my heart and give me the right words and spirit to articulate my belief.

December 12

> *And they which went before rebuked him,*
> *that he should hold his peace:*
> *but he cried so much the more,*
> *Thou Son of David, have mercy on me.*
>
> —Luke 18:39

Who am I to be so bold as to think I am special? I am a daughter of God, made in his image, and in his eyes I am perfectly special, just as each of us is. All I must do is look for my gifts and express them into the world!

December 13

Lynne's six-year-old daughter Phoebe has a severe peanut allergy, but the school Phoebe attends did not have any protocols in place should the girl experience an allergic reaction. At first, the school administration did not appreciate the severity of Phoebe's allergy, which is in fact life threatening. Lynne's initial efforts to bring attention to her daughter's condition were treated dismissively; she had to dig deep to be the firm, wise advocate her daughter's situation demanded. Dear Lord, please help me to be ready to speak up for those who cannot speak for themselves. May I be a wise and thoughtful advocate.

December 14

*And all they that were about them
strengthened their hands
with vessels of silver, with gold, with goods,
and with beasts, and with precious things,
beside all that was willingly offered.*

—Ezra 1:6

When everyone seems against us, we must remember
God is for us! Victory in life comes to those who
know that, no matter how many times our enemies
attack, we will win with God as our ally.

December 15

Even every one that is called by my name:
for I have created him for my glory,
I have formed him; yea, I have made him.

—Isaiah 43:7

Sometimes our children, spouses, family, and friends
take a toll on our energy. We feel we have given all we
have to give. This is the time to step away, get quiet
with God, and recharge the batteries so we can push
on through another day.

December 16

After a routine dental procedure went awry, Megan became very ill. She contracted blood poisoning and the pain in her jaw was beyond anything she'd ever experienced. Thanks to antibiotics and sound medical care, Megan recovered, but now, even months later, when she wakes pain-free she still gives thanks to God. "It took an extreme situation to remind me of the importance of thanking God; being grateful inspires joy, and I feel closer to God than ever," Megan says. Dear Lord, I understand how important it is to give thanks to you. It draws me closer to you, and is good for my heart.

December 17

Brethren, I count not myself to have apprehended: but *this* one thing *I do*, forgetting those things which are behind, and reaching forth unto those things which are before, I press toward the mark for the prize of the high calling of God in Christ Jesus.

—Philippians 3:13-14

Isn't it amazing how just trusting in God's power and grace can heal us? See it, know it, and heal it. What a gift we have been given!

December 18

And Saul said to David,
Thou art not able to go
against this Philistine to fight with him:
for thou *art but* a youth,
and he a man of war from his youth.

—1 Samuel 17:33

Dear Lord, Saul doubted that David could
overcome Goliath. But David did not let a
doubter—and a powerful one, at that!—stop
him from one of his greatest life achievements:
defeating Goliath. God, when others doubt
me, may I draw strength from David's story.

December 19

Selma's sister Heather had always enjoyed a glass or two of wine over dinner, but increasingly, Selma noticed that Heather was drinking in excess. Selma doesn't like confrontation, but things came to a head after an unpleasant, alcohol-fueled incident at a family dinner. With love and some trepidation, Selma sat down with Heather and encouraged her to seek treatment. It was a diffi cult, but necessary, conversation. Though tears were shed, Heather agreed to get help. Dear Lord, speaking the truth publicly is not always easy to do, but it is important. It is an act of love. Please help me to do so with strength and grace.

December 20

> But Moses' hands *were* heavy;
> and they took a stone, and put *it* under him,
> and he sat thereon; and Aaron
> and Hur stayed up his hands,
> the one on the one side, and the other
> on the other side; and his hands were steady
> until the going down of the sun.
>
> —Exodus 17:12

God, sometimes uplifting others means offering actual physical help. Please grant me the literal strength to be able to do so!

December 21

Study to shew thyself approved unto God,
a workman that needeth not to be ashamed,
rightly dividing the word of truth.
But shun profane and vain babblings:
for they will increase unto more ungodliness.

—2 Timothy 2:15-16

Dear God, may I not be distracted from my goals;
please help me to block out petty problems and gossip!

December 22

Though Tracy's mom is wheelchair-bound, she's still game for adventure. And Tracy, at 60, is grateful she still has the strength to take her mom out. "It can be a big production," Tracy says. "It'll be snowing, and getting my mom in and out of the car with the chair can be tiring. But I'm glad I can still do it: we go out for coffee at our favorite diner, or we'll go shopping together. It's always worth it!"

December 23

God puts friends in our lives to comfort us, support us, and share our burdens during dark times. And groups of friends can be powerful, indeed: Carrie, a single mom of two who lost her consulting job during an economic downturn, still remembers the solace provided by the prayer circle at her community church as she interviewed for a new position. "I knew others were thinking of me and praying for me," she shares. "It gave me strength."

December 24

Loving Father, help us remember the birth of Jesus, that we may share in the song of the angels, the gladness of the shepherds and the wisdom of the wise men. Close the door of hate and open the door of love all over the world. Let kindness come with every gift and good desires with every greeting. Deliver us from evil by the blessing which Christ brings and teach us to be merry with clean hearts.

December 25

I heard the bells on Christmas day
Their old familiar carols play,
And wild and sweet the words repeat
Of peace on earth, good will to men.
Then pealed the bells more loud and deep:
God is not dead, nor doth he sleep;
The wrong shall fail, the right prevail,
With peace on earth, good will to men.

—Henry Wadsworth Longfellow

December 26

Our hearts grow tender with childhood
memories and love of kindred,
and we are better throughout the year
for having, in spirit, become a child
again at Christmas-time.

—Laura Ingalls Wilder

Lord, how grateful we are that our spirits
don't have to sag once the excitement of
Christmas is over! We don't want to be like
ungrateful children tearing through a pile
of presents just to say, "Is that all?" For the
gift you gave us at Christmas, your beloved
son among us, is a gift that is ours all the
days of our lives and throughout eternity!
Thank you for the greatest gift of all, Lord.

December 27

Despite today's valley of shadow and sickness, I know you, shepherd of my soul, will continue restoring me as I move through treatment to the safe meadow of wellness.

December 28

Dear Lord, help me to tap into my inner spiritual
reservoir for strength. I know that strength is there!
I know you are there!

December 29

Lord, this time of year is a wonderful time for reflecting over the past year. Sometimes there is pain involved in looking back, but there is also so much joy and so many things that fill our hearts with gratitude. Renew our dedication to living a life that brings you glory for as long as we are on this earth. Remind us of the rich heritage that is ours through you, and keep us both humble and grateful.

December 30

Lord, sometimes it seems as if life is a series of good-byes. I know when I think this way I am focusing on the wrong part, though—for life can also be seen as a series of hellos! Even when the holidays are over and we go back to our regular, day-to-day lives, we come upon beautiful, exciting things every day. We just need to be on the lookout and ready to accept them into our lives. May I always be ready to accept blessing from you, Lord, whether they are large blessings that bowl me over or small blessings that I might miss if I'm too caught up in my own concerns.

December 31

> Healing is a matter of time,
> But it is sometimes
> also a matter of opportunity.
> —Hippocrates

For just as the harshest winter always gives way to the warm blush of spring, the season of our suffering will give way to a brighter tomorrow, where change becomes a catalyst for new growth and spiritual maturity, and we are able to move on with the joyfulness of being alive.